Governance in Flux

Policy Shifts on Planet Nebula

Morgan Bell

ISBN: 9781779666178
Imprint: Press for Play Books
Copyright © 2024 Morgan Bell.
All Rights Reserved.

Contents

Background of Planet Nebula

Planet Nebula, a vibrant and diverse world located in the Andromeda galaxy, has undergone significant transformations throughout its history. This section provides an overview of the foundational aspects of Nebulian society, including its formation, geographical features, and cultural diversity.

Formation and Development of the Society

The origins of Nebula can be traced back to a series of interstellar migrations approximately 5,000 years ago. Early settlers, drawn by the planet's rich resources and temperate climate, established small communities primarily along its vast river systems. These communities were characterized by tribal governance structures, where decisions were made collectively, often through consensus. This decentralized decision-making process fostered a sense of community, but also led to conflicts over resources, particularly during periods of drought.

As the population grew, so did the complexity of governance. The need for more structured leadership led to the emergence of chieftains who could mediate disputes and organize collective efforts. This transition marked the beginning of a more hierarchical society, culminating in the establishment of a centralized monarchy around 2,500 years ago. The monarchy, while providing stability, often struggled with legitimacy, as many citizens remained loyal to their local leaders.

Geographical and Environmental Features

Nebula is characterized by its diverse geographical landscape, which includes expansive forests, arid deserts, and towering mountain ranges. The planet's unique environment has played a pivotal role in shaping its society. For instance, the fertile river valleys have supported agriculture, leading to the development of trade networks among different regions.

Mathematically, the geographical distribution of resources can be analyzed using the following equation for resource allocation:

$$R = \frac{A \cdot P}{D} \tag{1}$$

Where:

- R = Resource availability

- A = Area of arable land

+ P = Population density

+ D = Distance to major trade routes

This equation illustrates how resource allocation is influenced by both environmental factors and societal needs.

Demographic and Cultural Diversity

The demographic landscape of Planet Nebula is a tapestry of various ethnic groups, languages, and traditions. The primary population centers are home to a mix of indigenous Nebulians and settlers from neighboring star systems. This cultural amalgamation has resulted in a rich mosaic of languages, art forms, and social practices.

Nebula's cultural diversity is exemplified by its festivals, which often celebrate historical events, agricultural cycles, or astronomical phenomena. For example, the Festival of Stars, held annually, honors the planet's celestial heritage, attracting visitors from across the galaxy. Such events foster a sense of unity among Nebulians while also highlighting the differences that enrich their society.

However, this diversity has not come without challenges. Ethnic tensions occasionally arise, particularly in regions where resources are scarce. The government has attempted to address these issues through policies promoting inclusivity and cultural exchange, though implementation has often been met with resistance from traditionalists.

Conclusion

In summary, the background of Planet Nebula is characterized by a complex interplay of historical development, geographical diversity, and cultural richness. The evolution from tribal governance to a centralized monarchy, followed by the emergence of democratic ideals, reflects the dynamic nature of Nebulian society. Understanding these foundational elements is crucial for analyzing the subsequent political, economic, and social reforms that have shaped the planet's governance in the modern era.

As we delve deeper into the historical overview of Nebula, it is essential to recognize how these foundational aspects have influenced the trajectory of its governance and policy-making processes.

Background of Planet Nebula

Planet Nebula, a celestial body located in the Andromeda Galaxy, is a fascinating case study of governance and societal evolution. Its unique geographical and environmental features, coupled with a rich tapestry of cultural diversity, have shaped the political landscape in ways that are both intriguing and complex.

Formation and Development of the Society

The formation of Nebula's society can be traced back to its early inhabitants, who were primarily nomadic tribes. These tribes relied on hunting, gathering, and later, rudimentary agriculture. As they settled in fertile regions, the need for organized governance became apparent. The initial governance systems were decentralized, characterized by tribal leadership, where decisions were made collectively in councils.

The transition from tribal leadership to more structured governance occurred as populations grew and resources became scarce. Conflicts over land and resources led to the emergence of stronger leaders, eventually culminating in a centralized monarchy. This shift marked a significant turning point in Nebula's governance, as it introduced hierarchical structures that prioritized control and stability over communal decision-making.

Geographical and Environmental Features

Nebula is characterized by diverse geographical features, including vast mountain ranges, sprawling forests, and extensive waterways. The planet's climate varies significantly across regions, influencing agricultural practices and settlement patterns. The northern regions are known for their harsh winters, while the southern areas enjoy a temperate climate conducive to year-round farming.

These environmental factors have not only shaped the economy but have also influenced the social fabric of Nebula. For instance, communities in the mountainous regions developed a culture of self-sufficiency, relying on livestock and trade with lowland tribes, while those in fertile valleys established more complex agricultural societies.

Demographic and Cultural Diversity

Nebula is home to a rich tapestry of cultures, languages, and ethnic groups. Over centuries, waves of migration and trade have introduced new ideas and practices, creating a multicultural society. The population is primarily divided into three major ethnic groups: the Aurans, known for their artistic expressions; the Terrans, who excel in agriculture and trade; and the Aquarians, whose expertise lies in navigation and fishing.

The coexistence of these diverse groups has led to both collaboration and conflict. Cultural festivals, such as the annual Unity Festival, celebrate this diversity, fostering a sense of community among the various groups. However, underlying tensions occasionally surface, particularly regarding resource allocation and political representation.

Theoretical Frameworks of Governance

The governance of Planet Nebula can be analyzed through various theoretical frameworks. One prominent theory is the Social Contract Theory, which posits that individuals consent to form a society and establish governance to protect their rights and welfare. In Nebula, this theory is particularly relevant as the transition from tribal to centralized governance reflects the collective agreement of the inhabitants to trade certain freedoms for security and order.

Another relevant framework is the Institutional Theory, which emphasizes the role of institutions in shaping social behavior. The evolution of governance structures on Nebula, from tribal councils to a centralized monarchy, illustrates how institutions adapt to meet the needs of society. The establishment of democratic institutions in the later stages of governance further exemplifies this adaptation, as the population sought to reclaim agency in decision-making processes.

Problems and Challenges in Governance

Despite its rich history, Nebula faces significant challenges in governance. The transition from a centralized monarchy to a democratic system has been fraught with difficulties. Issues such as political corruption, lack of transparency, and public disillusionment with elected officials have undermined trust in democratic institutions.

Moreover, the diverse demographic landscape poses challenges in terms of representation and inclusion. Marginalized groups often feel their voices are not heard, leading to social unrest and protests. The government's response to these challenges has been mixed, with some initiatives aimed at promoting inclusivity, while others have been criticized for being superficial and ineffective.

Examples of Governance in Action

A notable example of governance in action on Planet Nebula is the implementation of the "Nebulian Accord," a policy aimed at addressing income inequality and promoting social justice. This initiative was born out of grassroots movements advocating for the rights of marginalized communities. While the Accord has seen some success in redistributing resources and improving access to education and healthcare, it has also faced backlash from conservative factions who view it as a threat to traditional values.

Another example is the establishment of the Nebulian Council for Technological Advancement, which seeks to integrate scientific expertise into policy-making. This council has been instrumental in developing policies aimed at addressing climate change and promoting sustainable practices. However, public skepticism regarding the council's motives and the transparency of its operations has raised concerns about the potential for technocratic governance to overshadow democratic principles.

In conclusion, the background of Planet Nebula provides a rich context for understanding the complexities of governance in a diverse and evolving society. The interplay of historical developments, geographical features, and cultural diversity continues to shape the political landscape, presenting both opportunities and challenges for its inhabitants. As Nebula navigates its future, the lessons learned from its past will be crucial in informing effective governance strategies that prioritize inclusivity, transparency, and sustainability.

Geographical and Environmental Features

Planet Nebula is characterized by a diverse array of geographical and environmental features that have significantly influenced its governance, culture, and socio-economic development. This section will explore the various geographical attributes of Nebula, including its topography, climate, natural resources, and environmental challenges.

Topography

Nebula's surface is marked by a complex topography that includes towering mountain ranges, vast plains, intricate river systems, and expansive coastlines. The Nebulian Highlands, a prominent feature, are home to the planet's highest peaks, which rise to elevations of over 5,000 meters. These mountains not only serve as natural barriers but also influence weather patterns, creating microclimates that support diverse ecosystems.

The Great Nebulian Plain, situated at the heart of the planet, is a fertile area that has historically supported agriculture and settlement. The plains are interspersed with rivers, such as the River Nebulon, which plays a crucial role in irrigation and transportation. The river's seasonal flooding has historically provided nutrient-rich silt, fostering agricultural productivity.

Climate

Nebula experiences a range of climatic conditions, from arid deserts to temperate forests, influenced by its axial tilt and orbital position. The planet is divided into several climatic zones:

- **Tropical Zone:** Located near the equator, this region is characterized by high temperatures and significant rainfall, supporting lush rainforests and biodiversity.

- **Temperate Zone:** Found in the mid-latitudes, this zone experiences distinct seasons, with warm summers and cold winters. It is home to deciduous forests and agricultural lands.

- **Polar Zone:** The polar regions are marked by extreme cold and ice-covered landscapes. These areas are sparsely populated and have limited resources, presenting unique challenges for governance.

The climate of Nebula poses both opportunities and challenges for its inhabitants. For instance, the tropical regions offer rich agricultural potential, while the polar zones present difficulties in terms of habitation and resource extraction.

Natural Resources

Nebula is endowed with a wealth of natural resources that have shaped its economic landscape. Key resources include:

- **Minerals:** The mountainous regions are rich in minerals such as gold, silver, and rare earth elements. Mining has become a significant industry, contributing to the economy but also raising environmental concerns.

- **Forests:** The temperate and tropical zones are covered with vast forests, providing timber and non-timber products. However, deforestation has led to habitat loss and biodiversity decline.

+ **Water Resources:** The abundance of rivers and lakes is crucial for agriculture, drinking water, and industrial use. However, water management has become a pressing issue, particularly in arid regions.

The exploitation of these resources has led to economic growth but has also resulted in environmental degradation and social conflicts over resource allocation.

Environmental Challenges

Planet Nebula faces several environmental challenges that impact governance and policy-making:

+ **Climate Change:** Rising temperatures and shifting weather patterns threaten agricultural productivity and water availability. The government has implemented policies aimed at climate adaptation and mitigation, but public skepticism remains a barrier.

+ **Pollution:** Industrial activities and urbanization have led to significant air and water pollution, prompting public health crises. The government has struggled to enforce environmental regulations effectively.

+ **Biodiversity Loss:** Habitat destruction due to agriculture and urban expansion has resulted in the loss of native species. Conservation efforts are often hindered by political and economic interests.

In response to these challenges, Nebula has initiated various environmental policies, such as the Green Initiative, aimed at promoting sustainable practices and preserving natural ecosystems. However, the effectiveness of these initiatives is often undermined by competing economic interests and a lack of public engagement.

Conclusion

The geographical and environmental features of Planet Nebula are integral to understanding its governance and societal dynamics. The interplay between topography, climate, natural resources, and environmental challenges shapes the policies and political landscape of Nebula. As the planet continues to navigate the complexities of governance, addressing these geographical and environmental factors will be crucial for sustainable development and societal resilience.

Demographic and cultural diversity

Planet Nebula is characterized by a rich tapestry of demographic and cultural diversity, which has been shaped by its unique history, geography, and socio-economic developments. This diversity is not merely a statistic; it represents the complexities of governance, social cohesion, and economic development on the planet.

Demographic Composition

The population of Planet Nebula is approximately 7 billion inhabitants, comprised of various ethnic groups, languages, and religions. The major demographic groups include the *Zeltrons*, known for their vibrant cultural practices and communal living; the *Vortians*, who are predominantly urban dwellers with a strong emphasis on technological innovation; and the *Grythians*, a rural populace engaged in agriculture and traditional crafts.

The demographic distribution is uneven, with a significant concentration of the population in urban areas such as *Nebulopolis* and *Techno-City*, where opportunities for employment and education are more abundant. According to the latest census data, approximately 60% of Nebulans reside in urban centers, while the remaining 40% inhabit rural regions. This urban-rural divide presents challenges for governance, particularly in terms of resource allocation and access to services.

Cultural Practices and Beliefs

The cultural landscape of Planet Nebula is as diverse as its population. Each demographic group brings its own set of traditions, languages, and belief systems. The Zeltrons, for example, celebrate a festival called *Lumina*, which emphasizes community bonding and environmental stewardship. In contrast, the Vortians hold an annual event known as *TechFest*, showcasing innovations and advancements in technology.

Language is another critical aspect of Nebulian diversity. Over 200 languages are spoken across the planet, with *Nebulian Standard* serving as the official language for government and education. However, many communities continue to preserve their native tongues, which often serve as a source of cultural identity. The coexistence of multiple languages can lead to challenges in communication and policy implementation, particularly in education and public services.

CONTENTS

Challenges of Diversity

While diversity enriches the social fabric of Nebula, it also poses significant challenges for governance. One of the primary issues is the potential for ethnic tensions and conflicts. Historical grievances among different groups can resurface, particularly when resources are scarce or when political representation is perceived as inequitable.

For instance, during the *Great Resource Crisis* of 2045, competition for water resources between the Zeltrons and the Grythians escalated into protests and violent clashes. The government struggled to mediate the conflict, highlighting the need for inclusive governance structures that acknowledge and respect the rights and needs of all demographic groups.

Moreover, the disparities in socio-economic status among different groups further complicate the governance landscape. The Vortians, with their access to technology and education, often hold more political power compared to the Grythians, who may feel marginalized. This imbalance can lead to feelings of disenfranchisement and apathy towards the political process, undermining democratic principles.

Policies for Inclusion

To address these challenges, the Nebulian government has implemented several policies aimed at promoting inclusivity and social cohesion. The *Cultural Integration Act* of 2050 was established to foster dialogue and understanding among different groups. This act encourages cultural exchange programs, language preservation initiatives, and community-building activities.

Additionally, the government has made efforts to ensure equitable representation in political institutions. Proportional representation systems have been introduced to give voice to minority groups, allowing them to participate actively in the decision-making process. This approach has been met with mixed reactions; while some groups feel empowered, others argue that it has led to fragmentation and inefficiency in governance.

Conclusion

In summary, the demographic and cultural diversity of Planet Nebula is a double-edged sword. It presents both opportunities for vibrant social interactions and challenges for effective governance. As the planet continues to evolve, the need for inclusive policies that respect and celebrate this diversity will be paramount.

The lessons learned from Nebula's experiences can serve as valuable insights for other societies grappling with similar issues of diversity and governance.

$$D = \frac{N_e}{N_t} \times 100 \tag{2}$$

Where:

- D = Diversity Index

- N_e = Number of ethnic groups

- N_t = Total population

This equation illustrates the quantitative aspect of diversity on Planet Nebula, emphasizing the importance of recognizing and addressing the complexities that arise from a diverse population.

Historical Overview

Historical Overview

Historical Overview

The history of governance on Planet Nebula is a fascinating tapestry woven from the threads of its diverse cultures, geographical features, and socio-political dynamics. This historical overview aims to delineate the evolution of governance structures from their primordial roots to the complex systems that define Nebulian society today.

The Genesis of Governance

The origins of governance on Planet Nebula can be traced back to its early tribes, which emerged in response to the need for organization and cooperation among the disparate groups inhabiting its varied landscapes. These tribes were characterized by decentralized decision-making processes that relied heavily on consensus and communal leadership. The absence of formalized governance structures allowed for a fluidity in leadership roles, where individuals could rise based on merit and the respect of their peers.

$$\text{Decentralization} = \frac{\text{Local Autonomy}}{\text{Central Authority}} \tag{3}$$

This equation illustrates the balance of power that existed in early Nebulian societies, where local autonomy was paramount, and central authority was minimal. However, this system was not without its challenges. Conflicts often arose due to resource scarcity, territorial disputes, and differing cultural practices, highlighting the limitations of a purely decentralized governance model.

Transition to Centralized Monarchy

As the population of Nebula grew, so did the complexity of its social structures. The need for more cohesive governance led to the establishment of centralized monarchies. This transition marked a significant shift in the political landscape, as power became concentrated in the hands of a singular ruler or a small elite. The emergence of monarchy was often justified through the concept of divine right, where rulers claimed their authority was sanctioned by the cosmos itself.

The centralized monarchy introduced a more hierarchical structure, characterized by defined roles and responsibilities. However, this system also faced its own set of challenges, including corruption, abuse of power, and civil unrest. The Nebulian populace, accustomed to a degree of autonomy, began to resist the imposition of a rigid hierarchical order.

The Democratic Revolution

The discontent with monarchical rule laid the groundwork for a democratic revolution that would reshape Nebulian governance. Inspired by the ideals of equality and representation, various factions began to advocate for a system that would empower the citizenry. The revolution was marked by a series of protests and uprisings, culminating in the establishment of democratic institutions.

One of the key theoretical frameworks that informed this transition was the Social Contract Theory, as articulated by philosophers such as Jean-Jacques Rousseau. According to this theory, legitimate political authority arises from a contract between the governed and their rulers, emphasizing the importance of consent and accountability.

$$\text{Legitimacy} = \frac{\text{Consent of the Governed}}{\text{Authority}} \tag{4}$$

This equation encapsulates the essence of the democratic transition, wherein legitimacy is derived from the will of the people rather than divine sanction or hereditary right. The establishment of a constitution and the introduction of electoral processes marked significant milestones in the Nebulian journey toward democracy.

Challenges and Criticisms of Democracy

Despite the initial enthusiasm surrounding democratic governance, Nebula faced numerous challenges in its implementation. Issues such as voter apathy, manipulation of electoral processes, and the influence of money in politics raised questions about the effectiveness of democracy as a governing system. The rise of political factions further complicated the landscape, with parties often prioritizing their interests over the common good.

Critics of the democratic system pointed to the phenomenon of populism, where charismatic leaders exploited public sentiments to gain power, often undermining democratic principles in the process. The Nebulian experience echoed global trends, where democracies struggled to maintain their integrity amid growing polarization and disillusionment.

The Technocratic Era

In response to the challenges faced by democratic governance, Nebula entered what is referred to as the Technocratic Era. This period was characterized by a reliance on scientific expertise and data-driven policies. The technocratic approach sought to address the inefficiencies of democratic governance by prioritizing empirical evidence in decision-making processes.

The theoretical underpinnings of this era can be linked to the Rational Choice Theory, which posits that individuals make decisions based on maximizing utility. In the context of governance, this meant that policies were formulated based on quantitative analyses and statistical models, often sidelining the voices of the populace.

$$\text{Utility Maximization} = \sum_{i=1}^{n} \frac{\text{Benefit}_i}{\text{Cost}_i} \tag{5}$$

While the technocratic approach yielded some successes in terms of policy effectiveness, it also fostered public skepticism. Many Nebulians felt alienated from the decision-making process, leading to an erosion of trust in institutions. The gap between technocrats and the general populace became a focal point of contention, raising critical questions about the role of expertise in governance.

Conclusion

The historical overview of governance on Planet Nebula reveals a complex interplay of power dynamics, cultural shifts, and theoretical frameworks. From decentralized tribal systems to the challenges of democracy and the rise of technocracy, Nebula's journey reflects broader trends observed in human societies throughout history. As Nebulian society continues to evolve, the lessons learned from its past will undoubtedly inform the future of governance on the planet.

Early governance systems

Tribal leadership and decentralized decision-making

The early governance systems of Planet Nebula were characterized by tribal leadership and decentralized decision-making processes. In these societies, power was not concentrated in the hands of a single ruler or governing body; instead, it was distributed among various tribal leaders who represented different clans and communities. This section examines the principles of tribal leadership, the mechanisms of decentralized decision-making, the challenges faced, and examples from Nebula's history.

Principles of Tribal Leadership

Tribal leadership on Planet Nebula was founded on several key principles:

- **Collective Responsibility:** Leaders were chosen based on their ability to represent the interests of their tribes. This collective responsibility ensured that decisions were made with the consensus of the community, fostering a sense of unity and belonging.

- **Elder Wisdom:** Elders were revered as the custodians of knowledge and tradition. Their insights guided decision-making processes, reflecting a deep respect for history and cultural heritage.

- **Consensus Building:** Rather than relying on majority rule, tribal councils often sought unanimous agreement. This approach minimized conflict and reinforced social cohesion, albeit sometimes at the cost of efficiency.

Mechanisms of Decentralized Decision-Making

Decentralized decision-making in Nebula's tribal societies involved several mechanisms:

1. **Tribal Councils:** Each tribe held regular councils where leaders gathered to discuss pressing issues. These councils served as platforms for dialogue, negotiation, and the formulation of community policies.

2. **Community Assemblies:** Beyond tribal councils, larger assemblies were convened to address issues affecting multiple tribes. This broader participation allowed for diverse perspectives and collective problem-solving.

3. **Cultural Norms and Practices:** Decision-making was often guided by cultural norms, rituals, and traditions. These practices provided a framework for resolving disputes and making choices that aligned with community values.

Challenges of Decentralized Governance

Despite its strengths, decentralized governance on Planet Nebula faced significant challenges:

+ **Conflict Resolution:** The emphasis on consensus sometimes led to prolonged deliberations, hindering timely decision-making. In situations requiring swift action, the inability to reach agreement could exacerbate crises.

+ **Resource Allocation:** Disparities in resources among tribes created tensions. Wealthier tribes often had more influence in decision-making processes, leading to perceptions of inequity and favoritism.

+ **External Threats:** The lack of a centralized authority made it difficult to respond effectively to external threats, such as invasions or natural disasters. Coordination among tribes was essential but often challenging.

Examples from Nebula's History

Several historical events illustrate the dynamics of tribal leadership and decentralized decision-making on Planet Nebula:

+ **The Great Drought (Year 243):** During a severe drought, tribal councils convened to address water scarcity. The decision to share resources among tribes exemplified the power of collective action, though it also highlighted the challenges of equitable distribution.

+ **The Alliance of the Eastern Clans (Year 289):** Facing an external threat from a neighboring planet, several tribes formed an alliance. This collaboration demonstrated the potential of decentralized governance to unite communities for a common cause, albeit temporarily.

+ **The Festival of Unity (Year 305):** An annual event aimed at fostering cooperation among tribes showcased the cultural significance of unity. However, disputes over resource allocation during the festival led to tensions that underscored the fragility of decentralized systems.

Conclusion

Tribal leadership and decentralized decision-making were foundational elements of governance on Planet Nebula. While this system promoted inclusivity and cultural respect, it also encountered challenges that necessitated evolution. As Nebula transitioned to more centralized forms of governance, the lessons learned from its tribal past continued to influence its political landscape, shaping the future of governance in this vibrant society.

Challenges and conflicts in early governance

The early governance systems on Planet Nebula were characterized by a decentralized structure, primarily rooted in tribal leadership. This system, while promoting local autonomy and cultural diversity, also led to significant challenges and conflicts that shaped the political landscape of the planet.

Tribal Leadership and Fragmentation

The governance of early Nebulian societies was predominantly tribal, where each tribe operated independently with its own set of customs, leaders, and decision-making processes. This decentralized approach allowed for a high degree of local control and cultural expression. However, it also resulted in fragmentation, as tribes often competed for resources, territory, and influence. The lack of a unifying governance framework led to a scenario where inter-tribal conflicts became commonplace.

For example, the *Zyphor* and *Galdar* tribes, both located near the fertile *Zelith Valley*, frequently clashed over water rights and land usage. The disputes escalated to the point where both tribes engaged in skirmishes, leading to loss of life and a cycle of retaliation that further entrenched divisions. This situation exemplifies the inherent instability of a fragmented governance system, where competing interests often override collective well-being.

Challenges of Resource Allocation

Resource allocation presented another significant challenge in early Nebulian governance. With tribes competing for limited resources, decisions regarding distribution often led to favoritism and corruption among tribal leaders. The *Elders Council*, a group of respected leaders from various tribes, attempted to mediate resource disputes; however, their authority was often undermined by tribal loyalties.

The equation governing resource distribution can be modeled as follows:

$$R_i = \frac{T_i}{\sum_{j=1}^{n} T_j} \times R \qquad (6)$$

where R_i is the resource allocated to tribe i, T_i is the total claims made by tribe i, R is the total available resources, and n is the number of tribes. This formula illustrates the complexities of equitable resource distribution, where competing claims often resulted in dissatisfaction and conflict.

Internal Conflicts and Power Struggles

Internal conflicts within tribes were also prevalent, often arising from power struggles among leaders. As tribes grew in size and complexity, the role of leadership became increasingly contested. Charismatic leaders could gain significant followings, leading to factions within tribes that challenged traditional authority.

For instance, in the *Thalor* tribe, a faction led by a young leader named *Kara* sought to overthrow the elder chief, *Boros*. This internal strife culminated in a civil conflict that not only weakened the tribe but also made it vulnerable to external threats from rival tribes. Such internal conflicts illustrated how the lack of a cohesive governance structure could lead to fragmentation and instability, ultimately undermining the tribe's ability to function effectively.

Cultural and Ideological Conflicts

Cultural diversity, while a strength, also posed challenges in early governance. Different tribes held varying beliefs, customs, and practices, which sometimes led to ideological conflicts. The *Nerath* tribe, for example, held animistic beliefs that clashed with the more agrarian-focused *Varnok* tribe, which prioritized agricultural expansion over spiritual practices.

These ideological differences often manifested in conflicts over land use, with the Nerath tribe opposing the Varnok tribe's expansion into sacred lands. Such conflicts not only strained inter-tribal relations but also complicated efforts to establish a unified governance framework that could accommodate the diverse beliefs and practices of Nebulian society.

Conclusion

In summary, the early governance systems on Planet Nebula faced numerous challenges and conflicts stemming from fragmentation, resource allocation issues, internal power struggles, and cultural diversity. These conflicts not only hindered effective governance but also laid the groundwork for future political developments, ultimately leading to the transition toward more centralized forms of governance. Understanding these early challenges is crucial for analyzing the evolution of Nebulian society and its ongoing quest for effective governance.

Transition to a centralized monarchy

The transition to a centralized monarchy on Planet Nebula represents a pivotal shift in its governance structure, marking a departure from the previously decentralized tribal leadership that characterized the society's early years. This transition, which occurred over several centuries, was influenced by a multitude of factors, including social dynamics, economic pressures, and external threats that necessitated a more unified approach to governance.

Historical Context

Initially, Nebula was organized into various tribes, each governed by its own leaders, often chosen based on lineage, wisdom, or military prowess. This decentralized system allowed for a degree of local autonomy but also led to significant fragmentation and conflict among tribes. The lack of a cohesive governing body made it challenging to address common issues, such as resource allocation, defense against external threats, and inter-tribal disputes.

The early governance systems can be understood through the lens of social contract theory, which posits that individuals consent, either explicitly or implicitly, to surrender some of their freedoms and submit to the authority of a ruler or government in exchange for protection of their remaining rights. In Nebula's case, the persistent conflicts and resource scarcity prompted a collective desire for stability, which laid the groundwork for the emergence of a centralized monarchy.

Key Factors in the Transition

Several key factors facilitated the transition to a centralized monarchy:

* **Economic Pressures:** As the population of Nebula grew, the demand for resources increased. Competition among tribes for land and resources often resulted in violent confrontations. A centralized monarchy could more effectively manage resource distribution and mitigate conflicts, thus appealing to the tribes seeking stability.

+ **External Threats:** The rise of neighboring societies posed significant threats to Nebula's tribal factions. The need for a unified defense against external aggressors became paramount. A centralized authority could mobilize resources and coordinate military efforts more effectively than fragmented tribal leaders.

+ **Cultural Cohesion:** Over time, shared cultural practices and beliefs began to emerge among the tribes of Nebula. This cultural cohesion fostered a sense of identity that transcended tribal affiliations, making the idea of a centralized monarchy more palatable to the populace.

+ **Charismatic Leadership:** The rise of influential leaders who could unify disparate tribes under a single banner played a crucial role in the transition. These leaders often wielded significant personal charisma and military prowess, allowing them to gather support for a centralized authority.

Implementation of Centralized Monarchy

The actual implementation of a centralized monarchy involved a series of strategic moves by emerging leaders. These leaders often began by forming alliances with powerful tribes, promising protection and resource sharing in exchange for loyalty. Over time, they consolidated power by absorbing smaller tribes and eliminating rivals.

The transition was not without its challenges. Many tribes resisted the loss of autonomy, leading to conflicts that could be characterized as civil wars. However, the promise of stability and security often swayed public opinion in favor of the monarchs. The establishment of a legal framework, including codified laws and a system of taxation, further legitimized the monarchy's authority.

Theoretical Perspectives

From a theoretical standpoint, the transition to a centralized monarchy can be analyzed through various lenses:

1. **Max Weber's Theory of Authority:** Weber identifies three types of authority: traditional, charismatic, and legal-rational. The Nebulian monarchy initially drew on traditional authority, as tribal leaders transitioned into royal figures. Over time, however, as laws and bureaucratic structures were established, the monarchy began to embody legal-rational authority.

2. **Hobbesian Social Contract:** The transition can also be understood through the lens of Thomas Hobbes' social contract theory, where individuals

relinquish certain freedoms to a sovereign power in exchange for security and order. The chaotic tribal conflicts on Nebula mirrored Hobbes' notion of the "state of nature," where life was "solitary, poor, nasty, brutish, and short." The centralized monarchy promised a more ordered society.

3. **The Role of Institutions:** The establishment of institutions to support the monarchy—such as a standing army, a judiciary, and tax collection systems—was crucial. Douglass North's theory on institutions emphasizes that the rules of the game (or governance) shape the behavior of individuals and organizations. In Nebula, the creation of these institutions helped stabilize the monarchy's rule and reduce the likelihood of rebellion.

Challenges and Criticisms

Despite the advantages of a centralized monarchy, several challenges and criticisms arose:

- **Concentration of Power:** Critics argued that the concentration of power in the hands of a single ruler could lead to tyranny. The risk of abuse of power became a significant concern, particularly as some monarchs became increasingly authoritarian.

- **Neglect of Local Needs:** The centralized authority often struggled to address the diverse needs of different regions within Nebula. Local leaders and populations sometimes felt alienated from decision-making processes, leading to discontent and calls for greater autonomy.

- **Succession Issues:** The question of succession became contentious, with rival factions often vying for the throne. This internal strife occasionally resulted in violent power struggles, undermining the stability that the centralized monarchy sought to establish.

Conclusion

The transition to a centralized monarchy on Planet Nebula was a complex process driven by economic, social, and political factors. While it provided a framework for greater stability and resource management, it also introduced new challenges related to power dynamics and governance. Understanding this transition offers valuable insights into the evolution of governance structures and the delicate balance between authority and autonomy in any society.

$$\text{Centralized Authority} = \frac{\text{Stability} + \text{Security}}{\text{Resistance to Change}} \tag{7}$$

The Rise of Democracy

The Democratic Revolution

The democratic revolution on Planet Nebula marked a pivotal shift in the governance structure, transitioning from a centralized monarchy to a more participatory political system. This transformation was not merely a change in leadership but a profound societal awakening that redefined the relationship between the government and its citizens.

Historical Context

The roots of the democratic revolution can be traced back to a series of socio-political upheavals that began in the late 21st century. The Nebulian society, which had long been under the grip of a monarchial regime, faced increasing dissatisfaction among its populace due to widespread corruption, economic disparity, and lack of representation. The monarchy, characterized by an elite ruling class, struggled to address the needs of the diverse demographics of Nebula.

The combination of economic stagnation and social unrest catalyzed grassroots movements, which demanded greater accountability and transparency from their leaders. The emergence of these movements was fueled by a growing awareness of democratic ideals, largely influenced by global trends and the dissemination of information through emerging technologies.

Key Theoretical Frameworks

The democratic revolution on Nebula can be analyzed through various theoretical frameworks. One such framework is the *Social Contract Theory*, which posits that the legitimacy of authority arises from the consent of the governed. Philosophers like John Locke and Jean-Jacques Rousseau argued that individuals surrender some freedoms to a governing body in exchange for protection and the maintenance of social order. However, as the Nebulian monarchy failed to uphold its end of the social contract, citizens began to assert their rights, leading to demands for a new governance model.

Another relevant theory is *Participatory Democracy*, which emphasizes the importance of active engagement by citizens in political processes. The Nebulian revolution was characterized by a surge in civic participation, with citizens taking to the streets, organizing rallies, and utilizing social media platforms to amplify their voices. This shift towards participatory governance was instrumental in shaping the new political landscape.

Major Events and Milestones

The democratic revolution unfolded through several key events that galvanized public support and mobilized citizens. One of the most significant moments was the *March for Change*, a mass protest that took place in the capital city of Nebulon. This event saw thousands of citizens demanding an end to autocratic rule and the establishment of a democratic framework. The protest was notable not only for its size but also for its peaceful nature, showcasing the Nebulians' desire for reform without resorting to violence.

In response to the mounting pressure, the monarchy convened a series of dialogues with opposition leaders, which ultimately led to the formation of a *Constitutional Assembly*. This assembly was tasked with drafting a new constitution that would enshrine democratic principles and ensure the protection of individual rights. The assembly's work culminated in the adoption of the *Nebulian Constitution*, which established a parliamentary system of governance and introduced mechanisms for regular elections.

Challenges Faced

Despite the progress made during the democratic revolution, the transition was fraught with challenges. One of the primary issues was the entrenched power of the former ruling elite, who were reluctant to relinquish control. There were numerous instances of political maneuvering aimed at undermining the newly established democratic institutions. For example, the *Old Guard*, a faction of former monarchy supporters, attempted to influence the electoral process through misinformation campaigns and bribery.

Additionally, the lack of political experience among the newly elected officials posed significant challenges. Many of these leaders were activists with little understanding of governance, leading to inefficiencies and policy missteps. The initial years of democracy were marked by a series of political scandals and public disillusionment, as citizens began to question whether their voices were truly being heard.

Successes and Lessons Learned

Despite the hurdles, the democratic revolution ultimately set the stage for significant advancements in Nebulian society. The establishment of free and fair elections allowed for a more representative government, which in turn fostered greater public trust in political institutions. The inclusion of diverse voices in the decision-making process led to policies that better addressed the needs of various demographic groups, particularly marginalized communities.

One of the key lessons learned from Nebula's democratic revolution is the importance of civic education. As the revolution progressed, initiatives aimed at educating citizens about their rights and responsibilities became crucial. This emphasis on informed participation not only empowered individuals but also strengthened the democratic fabric of society.

Moreover, the revolution underscored the necessity of safeguarding democratic institutions from external and internal threats. The establishment of independent electoral commissions and anti-corruption bodies became vital in maintaining the integrity of the political system.

Conclusion

The democratic revolution on Planet Nebula was a transformative event that reshaped the political landscape and empowered citizens. While it faced significant challenges, the revolution ultimately laid the groundwork for a more inclusive and responsive governance structure. As Nebula continues to navigate the complexities of democracy, the lessons learned during this period remain relevant, serving as a reminder of the ongoing struggle for representation and accountability in governance.

Implementation of democratic institutions

The establishment of democratic institutions on Planet Nebula was a pivotal moment in the society's evolution, marking a departure from autocratic governance towards a system characterized by popular participation and representation. This section explores the theoretical foundations, practical challenges, and notable examples of democratic institution implementation on Nebula.

Theoretical Foundations

The implementation of democratic institutions is often grounded in several key theories of democracy, each providing a framework for understanding how governance can be structured to promote participation, accountability, and representation. Among these theories, the following are particularly relevant:

- **Liberal Democracy:** This theory emphasizes individual rights, the rule of law, and the protection of minority interests against the majority's will. On

Nebula, the adoption of a constitution enshrining these principles was a fundamental step in formalizing democratic governance.

+ **Participatory Democracy:** This approach advocates for direct involvement of citizens in decision-making processes. Nebula's early reforms included mechanisms for public consultations and referendums, allowing citizens to voice their opinions on critical issues.

+ **Deliberative Democracy:** This theory focuses on the importance of reasoned debate and discussion in democratic processes. Nebulian policymakers established deliberative forums where citizens could engage in informed discussions about policies, fostering a culture of dialogue.

Practical Challenges

Despite the theoretical underpinnings, the implementation of democratic institutions on Planet Nebula faced numerous challenges:

+ **Institutional Design:** Crafting institutions that effectively balance power among branches of government proved difficult. The initial design of the legislative body, for instance, faced criticism for either being too centralized or too fragmented, leading to inefficiencies in governance.

+ **Political Culture:** A legacy of tribal governance created a political culture that often favored informal networks over formal institutions. This cultural inertia posed a challenge to the acceptance and effectiveness of newly established democratic structures.

+ **Corruption and Accountability:** As democratic institutions took shape, issues of corruption emerged, undermining public trust. The lack of transparency in political financing and decision-making processes led to calls for reforms to enhance accountability mechanisms.

Examples of Implementation

Several key initiatives marked the implementation of democratic institutions on Planet Nebula:

+ **Constitutional Convention of 2045:** This landmark event involved representatives from diverse demographic and cultural backgrounds, ensuring that the resulting constitution reflected the values and needs of all

Nebulians. The convention's deliberations were broadcasted, fostering public engagement and support.

* **Establishment of the Electoral Commission:** To oversee fair and transparent elections, the Nebulian government established an independent Electoral Commission. This body was tasked with regulating campaign financing, monitoring electoral processes, and ensuring that all citizens had equal access to the ballot.

* **Decentralization Initiatives:** Recognizing the importance of local governance, Nebula implemented a series of decentralization initiatives that empowered regional councils. These councils were granted authority over local matters, enhancing citizen participation in governance and allowing for more responsive policymaking.

Outcomes and Reflections

The implementation of democratic institutions on Planet Nebula has yielded mixed outcomes. While significant strides have been made towards establishing a democratic framework, challenges remain. The interplay between established institutions and evolving political culture continues to shape the governance landscape.

$$\text{Democratic Effectiveness} = \frac{\text{Public Participation} \times \text{Institutional Integrity}}{\text{Corruption Level}} \quad (8)$$

This equation illustrates that the effectiveness of democracy is contingent upon both public engagement and the integrity of institutions, moderated by the level of corruption present. As Nebula navigates its democratic journey, ongoing efforts to enhance transparency, foster civic engagement, and adapt institutions to the needs of its citizens will be crucial for sustaining democratic governance.

In conclusion, while the implementation of democratic institutions on Planet Nebula represents a significant achievement, it is a dynamic process requiring continuous adaptation and vigilance. The lessons learned from Nebula's experience can serve as valuable insights for other societies seeking to navigate the complexities of democratic governance.

Challenges and criticisms of democracy

The rise of democracy on Planet Nebula, while celebrated as a significant advancement in governance, has not been without its challenges and criticisms. As the Nebulian society transitioned from a centralized monarchy to a democratic system, various theoretical and practical issues emerged that questioned the efficacy and sustainability of democratic governance.

Theoretical Foundations and Dilemmas

Democracy, as articulated by theorists such as Robert Dahl and John Rawls, is predicated on the principles of political equality and collective decision-making. However, these ideals often clash with the realities of governance. Dahl's concept of *polyarchy* emphasizes the need for inclusive participation, yet the actual implementation often leads to disenfranchisement of certain groups, particularly marginalized populations. This disparity raises questions about the authenticity of democratic representation.

Moreover, the *paradox of voting* illustrates a fundamental dilemma within democratic systems. According to the theory, rational individuals may choose not to vote if they believe their individual vote has a negligible impact on the outcome. This leads to lower voter turnout, undermining the legitimacy of elected representatives. In Nebula, this phenomenon has manifested in several elections, where participation rates dipped below 50%, leading to concerns about the representativeness of elected officials.

Populism and Polarization

The emergence of populist movements on Planet Nebula has further complicated the democratic landscape. Populism, characterized by the dichotomy between "the pure people" and "the corrupt elite," often exploits societal divisions and amplifies polarization. In Nebula, the rise of the *Progressive Coalition* and the *Conservative Movement* has led to a fragmented political environment, where compromise becomes increasingly difficult.

This polarization is exemplified by the contentious debates surrounding major policy reforms, such as the Green Economy initiative. Supporters of the initiative argue for urgent action against climate change, while opponents claim that such measures threaten economic stability. The inability to find common ground has resulted in legislative gridlock, raising concerns about the functionality of the democratic process.

Inequality and Access to Power

One of the most pressing criticisms of democracy in Nebula is the issue of socioeconomic inequality. Despite the formal structure of democratic governance, power remains concentrated among a small elite, often referred to as the *political class*. This elite influence is exacerbated by campaign finance systems that favor wealthy candidates and parties, leading to a situation where the voices of ordinary citizens are drowned out by the interests of the affluent.

The correlation between wealth and political power can be illustrated through the equation:

$$P = f(W, C)$$

where P represents political power, W represents wealth, and C represents connections. This function suggests that as wealth increases, so does political power, creating a feedback loop that undermines the core democratic principle of equal representation.

Disinformation and Erosion of Trust

In the age of technology, the proliferation of disinformation has emerged as a significant challenge to democracy on Planet Nebula. The role of social media in shaping public opinion has led to the spread of false narratives and conspiracy theories, which can distort electoral processes and erode trust in democratic institutions.

For instance, during the last presidential election, a series of viral misinformation campaigns targeted both major political parties, leading to confusion among voters and a subsequent decline in trust in electoral outcomes. The implications of this phenomenon are profound, as the legitimacy of democratic processes hinges on public trust. The erosion of this trust can be modeled by the equation:

$$T = \frac{C}{E}$$

where T represents trust, C represents credibility of information sources, and E represents the extent of electoral engagement. As the credibility of information sources declines due to disinformation, trust in the democratic process diminishes.

Conclusion

In conclusion, while democracy on Planet Nebula has provided a framework for political participation and governance, it faces significant challenges that threaten its integrity and functionality. The theoretical dilemmas of representation, the rise of populism and polarization, issues of inequality, and the impact of disinformation collectively highlight the complexities of maintaining a robust democratic system. As Nebula continues to navigate these challenges, it must seek innovative solutions to ensure that democracy remains a viable and effective form of governance for all its citizens.

The Technocratic Era

Embracing scientific expertise in governance

The governance of Planet Nebula has undergone significant transformations, particularly during the Technocratic Era, where a pivotal shift towards the integration of scientific expertise into policy-making was observed. This approach emphasized the reliance on empirical data and scientific methodologies to inform decisions, aiming to enhance the effectiveness and efficiency of governance.

Theoretical Framework

The theoretical underpinning of this movement can be traced to the principles of rational choice theory and evidence-based policy-making. Rational choice theory posits that decision-makers act in their self-interest, weighing the costs and benefits of various options to maximize utility. In the context of governance, this translates into the use of scientific data to inform policies that align with the collective interests of society.

Evidence-based policy-making extends this concept by advocating for decisions rooted in rigorous research and statistical analysis. According to [?], evidence-based approaches can lead to more effective governance outcomes, as they enable policymakers to make informed choices based on the best available evidence rather than political whims or anecdotal experiences.

Implementation of Scientific Expertise

The implementation of scientific expertise in governance on Planet Nebula involved several key strategies:

- **Establishment of Research Institutions:** The Nebulian government invested in the establishment of independent research institutions tasked with conducting studies on various societal issues. These institutions became the backbone of evidence-based policy-making, providing critical data and analysis to inform legislative processes.

+ **Data-Driven Decision Making:** Policymakers began to adopt data-driven approaches, utilizing statistical models and simulations to predict the outcomes of potential policies. For instance, the introduction of a new transportation policy was supported by predictive models that analyzed traffic patterns and environmental impacts, leading to more sustainable urban planning.

+ **Collaboration with Experts:** The government actively sought collaboration with scientists, economists, and sociologists to incorporate diverse perspectives into policy discussions. This collaborative approach facilitated a more comprehensive understanding of complex issues, from climate change to public health.

Challenges and Criticisms

Despite the advantages of embracing scientific expertise, several challenges emerged:

+ **Public Skepticism:** A significant portion of the Nebulian populace expressed skepticism towards scientific findings, often fueled by misinformation and distrust in institutions. This skepticism hampered the implementation of policies that relied heavily on scientific evidence, as citizens questioned the motives behind data interpretation.

+ **Political Interference:** The politicization of scientific data posed a substantial challenge. Politicians occasionally cherry-picked data to support their agendas, undermining the integrity of evidence-based policy-making. This phenomenon is exemplified by the contentious debates surrounding environmental regulations, where scientific studies were often misrepresented to sway public opinion.

+ **Ethical Concerns:** The reliance on data-driven decision-making raised ethical concerns, particularly regarding privacy and surveillance. The collection and analysis of vast amounts of data necessitated robust frameworks to protect individual rights and prevent misuse. The Nebulian government faced criticism for its handling of personal data, leading to calls for greater transparency and accountability.

Case Studies and Examples

Several notable case studies illustrate the impact of embracing scientific expertise in Nebulian governance:

+ **Public Health Initiatives:** During a health crisis, the government implemented policies based on epidemiological models that predicted the spread of disease. By analyzing data on transmission rates and population density, officials were able to enact timely interventions, such as targeted vaccination campaigns, that significantly reduced infection rates.

+ **Environmental Policy:** In response to escalating climate change threats, Nebulian scientists developed predictive models to assess the potential impacts of various environmental policies. The government utilized these models to formulate a comprehensive climate action plan, which included transitioning to renewable energy sources and enhancing conservation efforts.

+ **Economic Policy:** Economic reforms were guided by data analytics that identified sectors in need of investment. By focusing resources on industries with high growth potential, the Nebulian economy experienced a resurgence, demonstrating the effectiveness of data-driven economic strategies.

Conclusion

In conclusion, the embrace of scientific expertise in governance on Planet Nebula represents a paradigm shift towards rational, evidence-based decision-making. While challenges such as public skepticism and political interference persist, the benefits of informed policy-making are evident in various sectors. As Nebula continues to navigate complex societal issues, the integration of scientific knowledge will remain a cornerstone of effective governance, fostering a more resilient and adaptive society.

Policies driven by data and research

In the Technocratic Era of Planet Nebula, governance has increasingly relied on data and research to shape policies. This shift towards data-driven decision-making is rooted in the belief that empirical evidence can lead to more effective governance. The rise of big data analytics, coupled with advancements in computational technologies, has enabled policymakers to analyze vast amounts of information to inform their decisions.

Theoretical Framework

The theoretical underpinning of data-driven policies can be traced to the principles of evidence-based policy-making (EBPM). EBPM emphasizes the use of the best available evidence from systematic research in the decision-making process. According to [?], EBPM can enhance the effectiveness of public policies by ensuring that they are grounded in rigorous analysis rather than anecdotal evidence or political expediency.

The formula for EBPM can be expressed as follows:

$$P = f(E, C, A) \tag{9}$$

Where:

+ P = Policy outcome

+ E = Evidence from research

+ C = Contextual factors (social, economic, political)

+ A = Stakeholder actions and feedback

This formula illustrates that effective policy outcomes depend not only on the evidence itself but also on the context in which it is applied and the actions of stakeholders involved.

Implementation of Data-Driven Policies

The implementation of data-driven policies on Planet Nebula has manifested in several key areas, including healthcare, education, and environmental management. For instance, the Nebulian government established the Nebula Data Institute (NDI), which serves as a central repository for data collection and analysis. The NDI employs advanced statistical methods and machine learning algorithms to evaluate the impact of various policies.

Case Study: Healthcare Policy

A significant example of data-driven policy in Nebula's healthcare system is the introduction of predictive analytics to manage public health crises. By analyzing historical health data, the government was able to predict outbreaks of infectious diseases with remarkable accuracy. The formula used to predict the likelihood of an outbreak (O) can be expressed as:

$$O = \frac{I \times R}{D} \tag{10}$$

Where:

- I = Incidence rate of previous outbreaks

- R = Rate of population movement (migration patterns)

- D = Duration of previous outbreaks

This predictive model allowed for timely interventions, such as vaccination campaigns and public health advisories, ultimately saving lives and reducing healthcare costs.

Challenges of Data-Driven Policies

Despite the advantages of data-driven policies, several challenges persist. One significant issue is the quality and reliability of data. As noted by [?], poor data quality can lead to misguided policies and unintended consequences. For example, if the data used to inform a policy on education reform is outdated or incomplete, the resulting policies may fail to address current issues facing the educational system.

Moreover, there is a growing concern regarding data privacy and ethical considerations. The use of personal data for policy-making raises questions about consent and the potential for misuse. As highlighted by [?], the surveillance capitalism model can lead to a breach of trust between the government and its citizens, as individuals may feel that their personal information is being exploited for political gain.

Public Skepticism and Erosion of Trust

Public skepticism regarding data-driven policies has also emerged as a significant challenge. Many Nebulians express concerns that policies based solely on data may overlook the human element of governance. This skepticism can lead to resistance against policies perceived as overly technocratic or disconnected from the realities faced by citizens.

To combat this skepticism, it is essential for policymakers to engage with the public transparently and inclusively. As suggested by [?], participatory governance approaches can help bridge the gap between data-driven decision-making and public trust. By involving citizens in the data collection process and allowing them to provide feedback on proposed policies, governments can foster a sense of ownership and accountability.

Conclusion

In conclusion, while the shift towards data-driven policies on Planet Nebula presents numerous opportunities for enhancing governance, it also poses significant challenges. The reliance on empirical evidence must be balanced with ethical considerations and public engagement to ensure that policies are not only effective but also equitable and trusted by the citizenry. As Nebula continues to navigate the complexities of governance in the Technocratic Era, the lessons learned from its data-driven policies will be invaluable for shaping future governance strategies.

Public skepticism and the erosion of trust

The Technocratic Era on Planet Nebula heralded a new age of governance that prioritized scientific expertise and data-driven policies. However, this shift was not without its challenges, particularly regarding public skepticism and the erosion of trust in governmental institutions. As Nebulians encountered a complex array of policies and decisions made by experts, many began to question the motives and effectiveness of those in power.

Theoretical Framework

Public trust in governance is a critical component of a functioning democracy. According to the social contract theory, citizens grant authority to their leaders in exchange for protection and the promotion of their welfare. However, when this trust diminishes, the social contract is effectively broken. The erosion of trust can be understood through the lens of the *Trust-Confidence Model* (TCM), which posits that trust in institutions is influenced by three primary factors: competence, integrity, and benevolence.

The equation representing the TCM can be expressed as:

$$T = f(C, I, B) \tag{11}$$

Where:

* T = Trust in institutions

* C = Perceived competence of the institution

+ I = Perceived integrity of the institution

+ B = Perceived benevolence of the institution

In the context of Planet Nebula, the perceived competence of technocratic leaders was often undermined by instances of policy failure, leading to a decline in public trust.

Problems Contributing to Erosion of Trust

One significant problem contributing to public skepticism was the perception of technocrats as disconnected elites. As policies were increasingly formulated based on complex data analyses, many citizens felt alienated from the decision-making process. This disconnect was exacerbated by instances where policies did not align with the lived experiences of Nebulians, leading to feelings of disenfranchisement.

Additionally, the rapid pace of technological advancement created a knowledge gap. Many citizens lacked the expertise to critically engage with the data being presented to them, leading to a reliance on simplified narratives from media outlets, which often sensationalized or misrepresented the facts. This phenomenon is illustrated by the *Dunning-Kruger effect*, where individuals with limited knowledge overestimate their understanding, further complicating public discourse.

Examples of Erosion of Trust

Several incidents during the Technocratic Era exemplified the erosion of trust among Nebulians. One notable example was the government's handling of the environmental crisis caused by the rapid industrialization of the Green Economy. While the transition to renewable energy sources was lauded as a significant achievement, the accompanying pollution and displacement of communities led to public outcry. Citizens felt that their concerns were dismissed by technocrats who prioritized data over human impact.

Another example was the implementation of healthcare reforms. While the introduction of universal healthcare aimed to improve access, the initial rollout was marred by bureaucratic inefficiencies and technical failures. Citizens faced long wait times and inadequate services, leading to a perception that the technocratic leadership was out of touch with the realities of everyday life. Public forums and town hall meetings often devolved into heated debates, with citizens expressing frustration over their inability to influence policy decisions that directly affected their lives.

Consequences of Erosion of Trust

The erosion of trust had profound implications for Nebulian society. As skepticism grew, so did the popularity of populist movements that promised to return power to the people. These movements often capitalized on the disillusionment with technocratic governance, framing themselves as champions of the common citizen against an elite class of experts.

Moreover, the decline in public trust led to decreased political engagement. Voter turnout plummeted as citizens felt that their voices were not being heard. According to a study conducted by the Nebulian Institute of Political Science, voter turnout dropped from 75% to 50% in the span of a single election cycle, highlighting the disconnect between the government and its constituents.

In conclusion, while the Technocratic Era on Planet Nebula aimed to create a more efficient and data-driven governance model, it inadvertently fostered public skepticism and eroded trust in institutions. As Nebulians grapple with the consequences of this erosion, it becomes imperative for leaders to re-establish connections with their constituents, ensuring that policies reflect the needs and experiences of the populace rather than solely relying on expert opinion.

The Nebulian Political Landscape

The Nebulian Political Landscape

The Nebulian Political Landscape

The political landscape of Planet Nebula is a complex interplay of various ideologies, parties, and social movements that reflect the diverse interests and values of its inhabitants. This section examines the foundational theories that underpin Nebulian governance, the challenges it faces, and the unique characteristics that define its political environment.

Theoretical Frameworks

The governance structures on Planet Nebula can be analyzed through several political theories, including pluralism, elitism, and participatory democracy.

Pluralism posits that power is distributed among a variety of groups, each vying for influence over policy decisions. In Nebula, this is evident in the presence of multiple political parties, each representing different demographic and ideological constituencies. The Centrist Party, Progressive Coalition, and Conservative Movement exemplify this pluralistic approach, competing for voter support and attempting to shape the political agenda.

Elitism, on the other hand, suggests that a small group of elites holds the majority of power, often marginalizing the voices of ordinary citizens. This theory has relevance in Nebula, particularly during periods of technocratic governance, where scientific and economic elites have dominated decision-making processes.

The transition to a more democratic framework has aimed to address these imbalances, yet remnants of elitist influence persist in political discourse.

Participatory Democracy emphasizes the importance of citizen engagement in the political process. Nebula has witnessed a rise in grassroots movements that advocate for increased political participation and transparency. These movements challenge traditional power structures and seek to empower marginalized communities, thus reshaping the political landscape.

Challenges in the Political Landscape

Despite the rich tapestry of political ideologies, Nebula faces several challenges that complicate its governance:

Polarization is one of the most pressing issues, as political factions become increasingly entrenched in their positions. This polarization often leads to gridlock in the legislative process, hindering effective governance. The divide between the Progressive Coalition and the Conservative Movement, for instance, has resulted in significant clashes over social policies, economic reforms, and environmental regulations.

Misinformation poses another challenge, particularly in the age of digital communication. The role of social media in shaping public opinion has led to the spread of misinformation, complicating the electorate's ability to make informed decisions. This phenomenon has been exacerbated by the rise of echo chambers, where individuals are exposed primarily to viewpoints that reinforce their existing beliefs.

Voter Apathy also threatens the robustness of Nebulian democracy. Many citizens feel disillusioned with the political process, believing that their votes do not matter or that the system is rigged in favor of the elites. This apathy can lead to low voter turnout, undermining the legitimacy of elected officials and the policies they enact.

Examples from the Nebulian Political Landscape

The political landscape of Nebula is not merely theoretical; it is shaped by real-world events and examples that illustrate the dynamics at play:

The Great Debate of 2045   serves as a pivotal moment in Nebulian history, where citizens engaged in a nationwide dialogue about the future of governance. The debate highlighted the tensions between the technocratic elite and grassroots activists, ultimately leading to a series of reforms aimed at increasing transparency and citizen participation in decision-making.

The Rise of the Youth Movement   in recent years has also transformed the political landscape. Young Nebulians, driven by concerns over climate change and social justice, have mobilized to demand more progressive policies. Their activism has pressured established political parties to adopt more inclusive platforms, reshaping the priorities of Nebulian governance.

The 2050 Elections   showcased the evolving political landscape, with unprecedented voter turnout driven by grassroots campaigns and social media engagement.   The election results reflected a shift towards more progressive policies, signaling a potential realignment in Nebulian politics.

Conclusion

In summary, the Nebulian political landscape is characterized by a rich interplay of theories, challenges, and real-world examples. As the society continues to evolve, the dynamics of power, citizen engagement, and ideological competition will remain central to the ongoing discourse on governance. The future of Nebulian politics will depend on its ability to navigate these complexities while fostering an inclusive and participatory democratic process.

Political parties and factions

Centrist Party: The Moderates

The Centrist Party, commonly referred to as "The Moderates," has emerged as a significant political force on Planet Nebula, representing a blend of progressive and conservative ideologies. This party aims to appeal to a broad spectrum of the Nebulian electorate by advocating for balanced policies that address both economic growth and social equity.   In this section, we will explore the theoretical underpinnings of centrism, the challenges faced by the party, and notable examples of its policy initiatives.

Theoretical Framework of Centrism

Centrism is often defined as a political ideology that seeks to find a middle ground between extremes. According to political theorists, centrism can be characterized by the following principles:

- **Pragmatism:** Centrists prioritize practical solutions over ideological purity, focusing on what works rather than what aligns with a specific doctrine.

- **Inclusivity:** The Moderates strive to include diverse perspectives in the policymaking process, recognizing that a variety of voices can lead to more comprehensive and effective governance.

- **Compromise:** The ability to negotiate and reach agreements with other political factions is central to the Centrist Party's strategy, promoting stability and continuity in governance.

This theoretical framework positions the Centrist Party as a stabilizing force within the Nebulian political landscape, particularly in times of heightened polarization.

Challenges Faced by the Moderates

Despite its appeal, the Centrist Party faces several challenges in the current political climate:

- **Polarization:** As political polarization intensifies on Planet Nebula, the Centrist Party often finds itself squeezed between the more extreme positions of the Progressive Coalition and the Conservative Movement. This polarization can lead to a perception that centrists lack conviction or clarity in their policies.

- **Identity Crisis:** The Moderates frequently grapple with defining their identity. With members holding a range of views, from center-left to center-right, the party risks alienating constituents who seek a more defined ideological stance.

- **Electoral Viability:** In a political landscape dominated by two major factions, the Moderates must contend with the challenge of being seen as a viable alternative. This often translates into difficulties in securing funding and media attention, which are crucial for electoral success.

Policy Initiatives and Examples

The Centrist Party has undertaken several policy initiatives that reflect its commitment to balanced governance:

+ **Economic Stability Program:** In response to growing income inequality, the Moderates introduced an Economic Stability Program aimed at providing targeted support to low- and middle-income families. This program includes tax credits for working families and incentives for businesses that invest in local communities. The program's success is measured by its impact on reducing poverty rates and increasing disposable income among the target demographic.

+ **Healthcare Reform:** The Moderates advocate for a mixed healthcare system that combines public options with private enterprise. This approach aims to ensure universal access to healthcare while maintaining the efficiency and innovation often associated with private providers. The party's proposal includes a public option for those who cannot afford private insurance, alongside regulatory measures to control costs.

+ **Environmental Sustainability:** Recognizing the urgency of climate change, the Centrist Party has championed a Green Infrastructure Initiative. This initiative focuses on investing in renewable energy sources and sustainable public transportation systems. By promoting green jobs and reducing carbon emissions, the party seeks to balance economic growth with environmental stewardship.

Public Reception and Future Outlook

The public reception of the Centrist Party's initiatives has been mixed. While many Nebulians appreciate the party's pragmatic approach, others criticize it for lacking a bold vision. Polling data indicates that while the party has a loyal base, it struggles to attract undecided voters who may lean towards the more radical proposals of its competitors.

Looking ahead, the Centrist Party must navigate the complexities of an evolving political landscape. To maintain relevance, it may need to refine its messaging and strengthen its grassroots connections. By effectively communicating its successes and addressing the concerns of its constituents, the Moderates can position themselves as a viable alternative for Nebulians seeking stability amidst uncertainty.

In conclusion, the Centrist Party represents a critical component of Nebulian governance, striving to balance competing interests while promoting pragmatic solutions. As the political climate continues to shift, the party's ability to adapt and resonate with the electorate will determine its future role in the governance of Planet Nebula.

Progressive Coalition: The Reformists

The Progressive Coalition, often referred to as the Reformists, emerged as a significant political faction on Planet Nebula during the tumultuous Technocratic Era. This coalition represents a diverse group of citizens who advocate for progressive policies aimed at addressing social inequities, environmental challenges, and the need for a more inclusive democracy. With a focus on reforming existing structures, the Progressive Coalition seeks to create a society that prioritizes the well-being of its citizens over corporate interests.

Theoretical Foundations

The ideological framework of the Progressive Coalition is deeply rooted in principles of social justice, equity, and sustainability. Drawing from various theoretical perspectives, including social democracy and eco-socialism, the coalition emphasizes the importance of state intervention in the economy to rectify systemic injustices. The coalition's platform is influenced by the following theories:

+ **Social Justice Theory:** This theory posits that justice is not merely about the distribution of resources but also about ensuring that all individuals have equal access to opportunities and rights. The Progressive Coalition advocates for policies that dismantle systemic barriers faced by marginalized groups.

+ **Eco-Socialism:** This perspective combines ecological concerns with socialist principles, arguing that environmental sustainability cannot be achieved without addressing economic inequalities. The coalition supports initiatives aimed at transitioning to a green economy, emphasizing renewable energy and sustainable practices.

+ **Participatory Democracy:** The Progressive Coalition champions a model of governance that encourages active citizen participation in decision-making processes. This approach seeks to empower individuals and communities, ensuring that diverse voices are heard in policy formulation.

Key Policies and Initiatives

The Progressive Coalition has introduced a range of policies aimed at transforming Nebulian society. Some of the key initiatives include:

- **Universal Basic Income (UBI):** In response to rising income inequality, the coalition has proposed a UBI program that guarantees a minimum income for all citizens. This initiative aims to alleviate poverty and provide a safety net for those affected by automation and economic shifts. The formula for UBI can be represented as:

$$UBI = \frac{Total\ National\ Wealth}{Population} \tag{12}$$

  where Total National Wealth accounts for all economic resources available to the society.

- **Green New Deal:** The coalition advocates for a comprehensive Green New Deal that focuses on transitioning to renewable energy sources, reducing carbon emissions, and creating green jobs. This initiative aims to combat climate change while promoting economic growth.

- **Healthcare for All:** The Progressive Coalition supports the implementation of a universal healthcare system that guarantees access to quality medical services for all Nebulians. This policy addresses healthcare disparities and aims to reduce the financial burden on citizens.

- **Education Reform:** The coalition emphasizes the need for an equitable education system that provides quality education to all. This includes increasing funding for public schools, implementing vocational training programs, and ensuring access to higher education for underrepresented groups.

Challenges and Criticisms

Despite its ambitious agenda, the Progressive Coalition faces several challenges and criticisms:

- **Opposition from Conservative Factions:** The coalition's progressive policies have met significant resistance from conservative factions, particularly the Conservative Movement, which argues that such reforms threaten traditional values and economic stability. This opposition often manifests in political campaigns that frame reformist policies as radical or unfeasible.

+ **Implementation Difficulties:** The ambitious nature of the coalition's proposals raises concerns about their feasibility. Critics argue that the implementation of policies like UBI and the Green New Deal requires substantial financial resources and political will, which may not be achievable in the current political climate.

+ **Public Skepticism:** While the coalition has garnered support from progressive citizens, there remains a segment of the population that is skeptical of government intervention in the economy. This skepticism is often fueled by fears of increased taxation and government overreach, leading to a polarized public opinion on key issues.

Examples of Reformist Successes

Despite the challenges, the Progressive Coalition has achieved notable successes in various areas:

+ **Environmental Legislation:** The coalition successfully passed a series of environmental regulations aimed at reducing carbon emissions and promoting renewable energy. These regulations have positioned Planet Nebula as a leader in sustainable practices within the intergalactic community.

+ **Healthcare Access Expansion:** Following the coalition's advocacy, significant reforms were made to expand access to healthcare services, resulting in a marked decrease in uninsured rates across the planet. This success has reinforced the coalition's commitment to social welfare and public health.

+ **Grassroots Mobilization:** The coalition has effectively mobilized grassroots movements, empowering citizens to engage in activism and advocacy for progressive causes. This engagement has strengthened democratic participation and increased awareness of social justice issues.

Conclusion

The Progressive Coalition: The Reformists represents a critical force for change on Planet Nebula. By advocating for policies that prioritize social equity, environmental sustainability, and participatory governance, the coalition seeks to reshape the political landscape. While challenges remain, the coalition's successes demonstrate the potential for progressive reform to address the pressing issues facing Nebulian society. As the political landscape continues to evolve, the Reformists will undoubtedly play a pivotal role in shaping the future of governance on Planet Nebula.

Conservative Movement: The Traditionalists

The Conservative Movement on Planet Nebula, known colloquially as the Traditionalists, emerged as a significant political faction in response to the rapid changes brought about by the democratic revolution and subsequent policy shifts. This section delves into the ideological foundations, key challenges, and notable examples of the Traditionalists' influence in Nebulian governance.

Ideological Foundations

At its core, the Traditionalist movement is rooted in a desire to preserve the cultural, social, and economic values that have historically defined Nebulian society. The movement draws heavily on the works of prominent philosophers such as Edmund Burke, who emphasized the importance of tradition and gradual change over radical reform. The Traditionalists argue that a society's stability is contingent upon its adherence to established norms and practices, which they believe promote social cohesion and national identity.

The Traditionalists advocate for a governance model that prioritizes the following principles:

- **Cultural Preservation:** The movement emphasizes the importance of maintaining Nebulian customs, languages, and practices, viewing them as integral to the national identity.

- **Economic Protectionism:** Traditionalists often support policies that protect local industries from foreign competition, arguing that this approach safeguards jobs and promotes economic self-sufficiency.

- **Limited Government:** The movement favors a government that intervenes minimally in the lives of its citizens, advocating for personal responsibility and local governance.

Challenges Faced by the Traditionalists

Despite their ideological clarity, the Traditionalists have faced several challenges in the evolving political landscape of Planet Nebula:

+ **Demographic Shifts:** As younger Nebulians increasingly embrace progressive values, the Traditionalists struggle to attract a new generation of voters. The rise of multiculturalism and globalization has also led to a dilution of the Traditionalists' core message, making it more difficult to rally support.

+ **Internal Divisions:** The Traditionalist movement is not monolithic; it comprises various factions with differing views on social issues, such as immigration and climate change. These divisions often lead to infighting and weaken the movement's overall cohesion.

+ **Public Perception:** The Traditionalists are frequently portrayed in the media as out of touch with contemporary issues, particularly concerning social justice and environmental sustainability. This negative perception hampers their ability to connect with voters who prioritize these issues.

Notable Examples of Traditionalist Policies

The Traditionalists have implemented several policies that reflect their ideological beliefs, some of which have had significant impacts on Nebulian society:

+ **Cultural Heritage Laws:** In an effort to preserve Nebulian traditions, the Traditionalists have enacted laws that promote the teaching of local history and languages in schools. These laws aim to instill a sense of pride in Nebulian heritage among the youth.

+ **Trade Protectionism:** The Traditionalists have advocated for tariffs on imported goods, particularly in sectors such as agriculture and manufacturing. This policy is justified with the argument that it protects local jobs and promotes economic stability. However, it has also led to increased prices for consumers and tensions with trading partners.

+ **Limited Immigration Policies:** Traditionalist leaders have pushed for stricter immigration controls, arguing that an influx of foreign nationals threatens Nebulian jobs and cultural integrity. This stance has resonated with a segment of the population but has also drawn criticism for fostering xenophobia and social division.

Conclusion

The Conservative Movement, or the Traditionalists, remains a vital component of Nebulian politics, advocating for the preservation of cultural values and economic protectionism. However, the movement faces significant challenges, including demographic shifts, internal divisions, and public perception issues. As Planet Nebula continues to evolve, the Traditionalists must adapt their strategies to remain relevant in an increasingly progressive political landscape. Their future will depend on their ability to reconcile traditional values with the realities of a rapidly changing society, ensuring that they can effectively engage with younger generations while maintaining their core principles.

$$\text{Political Stability} = f(\text{Tradition, Economic Protectionism, Cultural Cohesion}) \tag{13}$$

In this equation, we posit that the political stability of Planet Nebula is a function of tradition, economic protectionism, and cultural cohesion as advocated by the Traditionalists. The challenge for this movement will be to balance these elements with the need for progress and adaptation in a globalized world.

Election and campaign strategies

Role of media and social media

The role of media and social media in the political landscape of Planet Nebula has evolved significantly over the years, shaping public opinion, influencing election outcomes, and redefining political engagement. As a multifaceted entity, the media serves as a conduit for information dissemination, a platform for political discourse, and a battleground for competing narratives.

Theoretical Framework

In understanding the role of media, we can draw upon the **Agenda-Setting Theory**, which posits that the media doesn't tell us what to think, but rather what to think about. This theory suggests that media outlets can prioritize certain issues, thereby shaping the public agenda. On Planet Nebula, this has been particularly evident during election cycles, where the media's focus on specific candidates or policies can sway public perception and voting behavior.

Another relevant framework is the **Framing Theory**, which examines how the presentation of information influences interpretation. For instance, a news report framing a political party's economic policy as "progressive reform" versus "government overreach" can lead to vastly different public reactions.

The Media Landscape

The media landscape on Planet Nebula is characterized by a diverse array of platforms, including traditional print and broadcast media, as well as digital and social media channels. The rise of social media has revolutionized the way Nebulians consume news and engage with political content. Platforms such as NebulaBook and TwitNebula allow users to share opinions, mobilize support for causes, and interact with political figures directly.

Challenges and Concerns

Despite the benefits of a vibrant media environment, several challenges arise:

- **Misinformation and Fake News:** The proliferation of unverified information on social media poses a significant threat to informed decision-making. For instance, during the last election, a viral post claiming that a candidate supported a controversial policy led to widespread outrage, despite the claim being entirely fabricated.

- **Echo Chambers:** Social media algorithms often create echo chambers where users are only exposed to viewpoints that reinforce their own beliefs. This phenomenon can polarize the electorate and diminish the potential for constructive dialogue.

- **Media Ownership and Bias:** Concentration of media ownership can lead to biased reporting and a lack of diverse perspectives. In Nebula, several major news outlets are owned by a handful of conglomerates, raising concerns about the impartiality of political coverage.

Impact on Political Engagement

The influence of media and social media on political engagement is profound. Social media campaigns have become pivotal in mobilizing voters, especially among younger demographics. For example, the Progressive Coalition successfully utilized social media platforms to engage with younger Nebulians, resulting in a significant increase in voter turnout among this age group during the last election.

Moreover, the role of influencers and public figures in shaping political discourse cannot be understated. Nebulian celebrities often use their platforms to advocate for social justice initiatives, thereby bringing attention to critical issues and encouraging civic participation.

Conclusion

In conclusion, the media and social media play a crucial role in the political landscape of Planet Nebula, acting as both a facilitator of democracy and a source of challenges. As Nebulians navigate the complexities of information in the digital age, the need for media literacy and critical engagement with political content becomes increasingly vital. The ongoing evolution of media will undoubtedly continue to shape the governance and political dynamics on Planet Nebula for years to come.

Voter demographic analysis

The analysis of voter demographics on Planet Nebula is crucial for understanding electoral behavior, policy preferences, and the overall political landscape. This section delves into the various demographic factors that influence voter turnout and preferences, including age, gender, socioeconomic status, education, and geographic location.

Demographic Factors Influencing Voter Turnout

Voter turnout is often influenced by a combination of demographic characteristics. Research suggests that certain groups are more likely to participate in elections than others. For instance, older Nebulians tend to vote at higher rates compared to their younger counterparts. According to the Nebulian Electoral Commission (NEC), voter turnout among citizens aged 65 and older reached 78% in the last election cycle, while turnout for those aged 18-24 was only 42%. This trend aligns with the *Civic Voluntarism Model*, which posits that older individuals are more likely to engage in civic activities due to accumulated resources and a stronger sense of civic duty.

Gender and Voting Patterns

Gender also plays a significant role in voting behavior. Recent studies indicate that female Nebulians are increasingly mobilizing and participating in elections. In the last election, women accounted for 52% of the total voter turnout, a notable increase from previous years. This shift can be attributed to the rise of grassroots movements advocating for women's rights and representation, such as the *Nebulian Women's Coalition*. Data from the NEC reveals that women voters tend to prioritize social issues, such as healthcare and education, more than their male counterparts, who often emphasize economic concerns.

Socioeconomic Status and Political Preferences

Socioeconomic status is another critical factor influencing voter behavior. Nebulians from lower-income brackets are often underrepresented in the electoral process. A survey conducted by the *Institute for Nebulian Studies* found that only 35% of individuals earning below the Nebulian Median Income (NMI) participated in the last election, compared to 70% of those earning above the NMI. This disparity can be explained by barriers such as lack of access to information, transportation issues, and feelings of disenfranchisement.

To quantify this relationship, we can use the following logistic regression model:

$$P(Y = 1|X) = \frac{1}{1 + e^{-(\beta_0 + \beta_1 \text{Income} + \beta_2 \text{Education} + \beta_3 \text{Age} + \beta_4 \text{Gender})}} \quad (14)$$

Where $P(Y = 1|X)$ represents the probability of voting, X includes income, education, age, and gender as independent variables, and β_0 is the intercept term.

Education and Political Engagement

Education is another significant predictor of voter turnout. Higher levels of education correlate with increased political engagement. Data indicates that Nebulians with a tertiary education have a voting rate of 85%, compared to just 50% among those with only a primary education. The *Knowledge Gap Hypothesis* suggests that individuals with higher education levels are more likely to seek out information and understand the political process, leading to greater participation.

Geographic Variations in Voting Behavior

Geographic location also affects voter demographics. Urban areas, characterized by their diverse populations and higher concentrations of younger voters, tend to lean more towards progressive policies. In contrast, rural areas often exhibit conservative tendencies. For instance, the city of Nebulopolis reported a 65% turnout rate with a strong preference for the Progressive Coalition, while the rural district of Dusty Plains saw a turnout of only 45%, favoring the Conservative Movement.

Challenges in Voter Demographic Analysis

Despite the wealth of data available, several challenges persist in accurately analyzing voter demographics. One significant issue is the underreporting of certain demographic groups, particularly minority populations and lower-income citizens. The NEC has acknowledged that traditional survey methods may not capture the full spectrum of voter demographics, leading to skewed results.

Moreover, the rise of social media has transformed the landscape of political engagement, complicating demographic analysis. The *Digital Divide* refers to the gap between those who have access to digital technologies and those who do not. Nebulians in remote areas may lack reliable internet access, inhibiting their ability to engage in online political discussions or access vital voting information.

Conclusion

In conclusion, the demographic analysis of Nebulian voters reveals significant trends and challenges that shape the political landscape. Understanding these factors is essential for political parties and candidates as they develop strategies to engage with diverse voter populations. Future research should focus on overcoming the barriers to participation faced by underrepresented groups and leveraging technology to enhance voter engagement across all demographics. By addressing these issues, Planet Nebula can strive towards a more inclusive and representative democratic process.

Funding and campaign finance regulations

In the political landscape of Planet Nebula, the financing of electoral campaigns has emerged as a pivotal issue influencing the integrity of democratic processes. The regulation of campaign financing is essential to ensure fair competition among candidates and to maintain public trust in the electoral system. This section delves into the theoretical underpinnings of campaign finance, the challenges faced in regulating funding, and examples from Nebula's political history.

Theoretical Framework

Campaign finance theory posits that the funding of political campaigns can significantly affect electoral outcomes and the representation of diverse interests. The two primary theories guiding campaign finance regulation are:

+ **The Pluralist Theory:** This theory suggests that a multitude of interest groups compete for influence in the political arena. Campaign financing is viewed as a means for these groups to amplify their voices. As such, a regulated funding environment can ensure that no single group dominates the discourse, fostering a more representative political landscape.

+ **The Elite Theory:** In contrast, this theory posits that political power is concentrated in the hands of a few wealthy individuals or corporations. Under this view, unregulated campaign financing can lead to a system where the interests of the elite overshadow those of the general populace, thereby undermining the democratic process.

The balance between these two theories informs the ongoing debate about the necessity and effectiveness of campaign finance regulations.

Challenges in Regulation

Despite the theoretical frameworks advocating for regulation, Planet Nebula faces several challenges in implementing effective campaign finance laws:

+ **Lack of Transparency:** One of the primary issues is the opacity surrounding campaign contributions. Many candidates receive funding from anonymous sources, making it difficult to ascertain the influence of specific donors on political decisions. This lack of transparency can lead to public distrust and allegations of corruption.

+ **Influence of Super PACs:** Super Political Action Committees (Super PACs) have emerged as powerful entities that can raise unlimited funds to support or oppose candidates. While they are required to operate independently of candidates, the lines often blur, leading to concerns about undue influence over electoral outcomes.

+ **Legal Loopholes:** Existing campaign finance laws may contain loopholes that allow for circumvention. For instance, contributions can be funneled through multiple entities or disguised as donations to ostensibly independent organizations, complicating the enforcement of regulations.

Examples from Nebula's Political History

The historical context of campaign financing on Planet Nebula provides valuable insights into the consequences of both regulated and unregulated funding:

+ **The 2200 Elections:** During the elections of 2200, a significant scandal emerged when it was revealed that a major corporation had secretly funded multiple candidates across various parties. This led to widespread public outrage and calls for stricter regulations. In response, the Nebulian government instituted the *Transparency in Campaign Financing Act*, which mandated full disclosure of all campaign contributions above a certain threshold.

+ **The Rise of Grassroots Movements:** In contrast, the 2225 elections saw the rise of grassroots movements that successfully funded their campaigns through small donations from a large number of supporters. This shift demonstrated that with effective regulations, candidates could compete without relying on large corporate donations, thereby enhancing democratic participation.

+ **Ongoing Debates:** The debate surrounding campaign finance continues to evolve. Recent proposals to impose limits on individual contributions have faced opposition from those who argue that such restrictions infringe on free speech rights, as articulated in the Nebulian Constitution. This ongoing tension between regulation and freedom of expression remains a central theme in Nebula's political discourse.

Conclusion

The regulation of campaign financing on Planet Nebula is a complex issue that intertwines with the very fabric of its democratic values. While the theoretical frameworks provide a foundation for understanding the implications of campaign finance, the practical challenges and historical examples highlight the need for ongoing reform and vigilance. As Nebula continues to navigate the intricacies of funding and campaign finance regulations, the lessons learned from its past will be crucial in shaping a more equitable political future.

$$F = \frac{C}{D} \tag{15}$$

Where F represents the fairness of the electoral process, C is the total campaign contributions, and D is the degree of transparency in funding sources. A higher value of F indicates a more equitable electoral landscape, emphasizing the importance of rigorous campaign finance regulations.

Public Opinion and Political Engagement

Opinion polls and their impact on policy decisions

Opinion polls have become an integral part of the political landscape on Planet Nebula, influencing not only public perception but also the decision-making processes of policymakers. These polls serve as a barometer for the sentiments of the populace, providing insights into the preferences, priorities, and concerns of Nebulians. However, the relationship between opinion polls and policy decisions is complex and multifaceted, often leading to both positive and negative consequences.

Theoretical Framework

At the core of understanding the impact of opinion polls on policy decisions lies the concept of *public opinion*. Public opinion can be defined as the collective attitudes and beliefs of individuals on specific issues, which can be quantified through systematic polling methods. Theories of public opinion suggest that it plays a crucial role in shaping political behavior and governance. According to the *Spiral of Silence Theory*, individuals may withhold their opinions if they perceive themselves to be in the minority, leading to a skewed representation of public sentiment in polls.

Moreover, the *Agenda-Setting Theory* posits that media coverage of opinion polls can influence the public agenda by highlighting certain issues over others. This interplay between media, public opinion, and policymaking underscores the importance of opinion polls in the governance framework of Nebula.

Impact on Policy Decisions

The impact of opinion polls on policy decisions in Nebula can be observed through several key mechanisms:

1. **Shaping Policy Agenda:** Opinion polls often dictate which issues are prioritized by policymakers. For instance, during the recent energy crisis, polls indicated a significant public demand for renewable energy solutions. In response, the government accelerated its transition to green energy policies, illustrating how public sentiment can directly influence legislative priorities.

2. **Legitimizing Policy Choices:** Policymakers frequently use opinion polls to justify their decisions. When a controversial policy is proposed,

demonstrating that a majority of the population supports it can provide the necessary political cover. For example, the implementation of universal healthcare was backed by polls showing over 70% of Nebulians in favor, allowing the government to navigate opposition more effectively.

3. **Feedback Mechanism:** Opinion polls serve as a feedback mechanism for policymakers. By regularly gauging public sentiment, leaders can adjust their policies to better align with the expectations of their constituents. This was evident during the recent education reforms, where continuous polling revealed dissatisfaction with the proposed changes, prompting the government to revise its approach.

4. **Voter Mobilization:** Political parties and candidates utilize opinion polls to strategize their campaigns and mobilize voters. For instance, the Progressive Coalition, recognizing a surge in public support for social justice initiatives, tailored its campaign messages to resonate with these sentiments, ultimately leading to a significant electoral victory.

Challenges and Criticisms

Despite their usefulness, opinion polls are not without challenges and criticisms. One significant concern is the *accuracy* of polls. Factors such as sampling bias, question wording, and timing can skew results, leading to misinterpretations of public sentiment. For example, a poll conducted just days before a major election may not accurately reflect the views of undecided voters who may change their minds at the last minute.

Additionally, the reliance on opinion polls can lead to *populism*, where policymakers prioritize popular opinion over expert advice or long-term considerations. This can result in short-sighted policies that may not address the underlying issues facing society. An example of this was the backlash against immigration policies that were initially popular but later resulted in significant social unrest and economic challenges.

Case Studies

To illustrate the impact of opinion polls on policy decisions, consider two notable case studies from Planet Nebula:

Case Study 1: The Renewable Energy Transition In the wake of environmental degradation and energy shortages, a series of opinion polls revealed a growing public demand for renewable energy sources. The government, responding to this clear mandate, implemented aggressive policies aimed at transitioning from fossil fuels to renewable energy. This shift not only aligned with public sentiment but also positioned Nebula as a leader in sustainable practices, showcasing the positive impact of opinion polls on effective governance.

Case Study 2: The Healthcare Debate During the contentious debate over healthcare reform, opinion polls indicated a stark divide among Nebulians. While a significant portion supported universal healthcare, a vocal minority opposed it due to fears of increased taxation. The government faced a dilemma: to proceed with the reform, risking alienation of the opposing faction, or to cater to public apprehensions. Ultimately, the administration chose to implement a phased approach, using polling data to refine its messaging and address concerns, demonstrating how opinion polls can guide nuanced policy development.

Conclusion

In conclusion, opinion polls on Planet Nebula play a critical role in shaping policy decisions, acting as both a reflection of public sentiment and a tool for political strategy. While they offer valuable insights into the preferences of Nebulians, the potential for misinterpretation and the risk of populism underscore the need for a balanced approach. Policymakers must navigate the complexities of public opinion with caution, ensuring that decisions are informed not only by polling data but also by expert analysis and long-term vision. As Nebula continues to evolve, the interplay between opinion polls and governance will remain a pivotal aspect of its political landscape.

Grassroots movements and citizen activism

Grassroots movements and citizen activism have become pivotal forces in shaping political landscapes on Planet Nebula. These movements, often initiated at the community level, mobilize citizens to advocate for change, influence policy, and hold governments accountable. This section explores the theoretical foundations, challenges, and significant examples of grassroots activism in Nebula's political context.

Theoretical Foundations

Grassroots movements are typically characterized by their bottom-up approach, contrasting with top-down political structures. The theory of participatory democracy underpins many grassroots initiatives, advocating for increased citizen involvement in political decision-making processes. According to [?], participatory democracy enhances political legitimacy and fosters a sense of community ownership over governance.

Furthermore, social movement theory provides a framework for understanding how collective action emerges from shared grievances. [?] posits that social movements arise when individuals identify common interests and organize to challenge existing power structures. Grassroots movements often utilize strategies such as protests, petitions, and community organizing to amplify their voices and demand change.

Challenges Faced by Grassroots Movements

Despite their potential to effect change, grassroots movements on Planet Nebula face several challenges. One significant issue is the fragmentation of movements, which can dilute their impact. As noted by [?], when various groups pursue similar goals but operate independently, it can lead to competition for resources and public attention, ultimately undermining their collective effectiveness.

Moreover, the role of technology in grassroots activism presents both opportunities and challenges. While social media platforms can facilitate organization and mobilization, they can also lead to misinformation and polarization. The rapid dissemination of information can result in the spread of false narratives, complicating the efforts of activists to present coherent and unified messages.

Examples of Successful Grassroots Movements

Several grassroots movements have emerged on Planet Nebula, each highlighting the power of citizen activism. One notable example is the *Nebulian Youth for Climate Action*, a coalition of young activists advocating for sustainable environmental policies. The movement gained momentum following a series of climate-related disasters, prompting citizens to demand immediate action from their leaders. Through organized protests and social media campaigns, they successfully pressured the Nebulian government to adopt more aggressive climate policies, including a commitment to achieve net-zero carbon emissions by 2040.

Another significant example is the *Equality for All Movement*, which emerged in response to widespread discrimination against marginalized communities. This movement successfully lobbied for the implementation of anti-discrimination laws and policies aimed at promoting social justice. Utilizing grassroots organizing techniques, such as community forums and coalition-building, the movement garnered widespread support and ultimately influenced legislative changes that improved the rights and representation of underrepresented groups.

The Role of Technology in Activism

The advent of digital technologies has transformed the landscape of grassroots activism on Planet Nebula. Social media platforms serve as critical tools for mobilization, allowing activists to reach broader audiences and coordinate actions in real-time. However, this reliance on technology also raises concerns about data privacy and surveillance. Activists must navigate the delicate balance between leveraging technology for advocacy and protecting their personal information from potential government scrutiny.

Furthermore, the phenomenon of online activism, or "slacktivism," poses a challenge to the effectiveness of grassroots movements. While online engagement can raise awareness, it often lacks the tangible impact of traditional activism. [?] argues that the ease of online participation can lead to a false sense of accomplishment, where individuals feel they have contributed to a cause without engaging in more substantive actions.

Conclusion

Grassroots movements and citizen activism play a crucial role in shaping the political landscape of Planet Nebula. By leveraging the principles of participatory democracy and collective action, citizens can challenge existing power structures and advocate for meaningful change. However, these movements must navigate various challenges, including fragmentation, the impact of technology, and the risk of complacency. As the political climate continues to evolve, the resilience and adaptability of grassroots activism will be essential in addressing the pressing issues facing Nebulian society.

Public perception of political leaders and institutions

Public perception of political leaders and institutions is a critical aspect of governance on Planet Nebula. It encompasses the beliefs, attitudes, and evaluations that citizens hold towards their leaders and the governing bodies that shape their lives. Understanding these perceptions is vital for assessing the legitimacy of the political system and the effectiveness of governance.

Theoretical Framework

Theories of political perception often draw on social psychology and political science. One prominent framework is the *Social Identity Theory*, which posits that individuals derive a sense of self from their group memberships, influencing their perceptions of leaders based on how well those leaders represent their identity groups (Tajfel & Turner, 1979). This can lead to in-group favoritism, where citizens perceive leaders from their own demographic or political group more favorably, potentially skewing public opinion.

Another relevant theory is the *Public Trust Theory*, which suggests that trust in political leaders and institutions is essential for effective governance (Mishler & Rose, 2001). High levels of public trust can enhance cooperation and compliance with laws and policies, while low trust can lead to disengagement and dissent.

Factors Influencing Public Perception

Several factors influence public perception of political leaders and institutions on Planet Nebula:

- **Media Representation:** The portrayal of leaders in traditional and social media significantly shapes public perception. For instance, a study conducted during the recent election cycle revealed that candidates who received positive media coverage enjoyed a 20% higher approval rating compared to those who faced negative press (Nebulian Media Institute, 2023).

- **Performance and Accountability:** Citizens often evaluate leaders based on their performance in office. Metrics such as economic growth, unemployment rates, and public health outcomes serve as benchmarks. For example, the administration's handling of the pandemic led to a 15% drop in approval ratings when healthcare systems were overwhelmed, demonstrating a direct correlation between performance and public perception.

- **Crisis Response:** The ability of leaders to respond effectively to crises can significantly impact public perception. During the recent natural disaster, leaders who communicated transparently and acted decisively saw their approval ratings increase by 25% (Crisis Management Research Group, 2023). In contrast, leaders perceived as indecisive or evasive faced severe backlash.

+ **Cultural and Demographic Factors:** Cultural values and demographic characteristics, such as age, education, and socioeconomic status, also play a role. Younger Nebulians tend to favor progressive leaders who advocate for social justice, while older citizens may prefer traditionalists who emphasize stability and security.

Challenges in Public Perception

Despite the importance of public perception, several challenges complicate its landscape on Planet Nebula:

+ **Misinformation and Disinformation:** The rise of social media has facilitated the spread of misinformation, creating confusion and distrust among the populace. A survey indicated that 40% of Nebulians reported encountering false information about political leaders, which negatively affected their perceptions (Nebulian Institute for Research, 2023).

+ **Polarization:** The political landscape has become increasingly polarized, with citizens often viewing opposing leaders through a lens of skepticism and hostility. This polarization can lead to a phenomenon known as *confirmation bias*, where individuals only seek out information that reinforces their existing beliefs, further entrenching negative perceptions of rival leaders.

+ **Erosion of Trust:** Continuous scandals and perceived corruption have eroded trust in political institutions. The recent corruption scandal involving high-ranking officials resulted in a 30% drop in trust in the government, demonstrating how scandals can have lasting impacts on public perception (Transparency Nebula, 2023).

Examples of Public Perception Dynamics

To illustrate the dynamics of public perception, consider the case of President Zorath, who faced a significant crisis during a severe economic downturn. Initially, Zorath's approval ratings were high due to effective crisis management. However, as economic conditions worsened, public perception shifted dramatically. The following equation illustrates this relationship:

$$P = \alpha E - \beta C + \gamma T$$

where:

+ P = Public perception score

+ E = Economic performance index

+ C = Crisis management effectiveness score

+ T = Trust in political institutions score

+ α, β, γ = Coefficients representing the weight of each factor

In this case, as E declined and C became negative due to ineffective responses, P also dropped, highlighting the interplay of these factors in shaping public perception.

Conclusion

In conclusion, public perception of political leaders and institutions on Planet Nebula is shaped by a complex interplay of media representation, performance, crisis response, and demographic factors. However, challenges such as misinformation, polarization, and erosion of trust pose significant barriers to positive public perception. Understanding these dynamics is crucial for leaders aiming to maintain legitimacy and effectively govern in an increasingly complex political landscape. As Nebulian society continues to evolve, so too will the perceptions of its leaders and institutions, underscoring the need for ongoing dialogue and engagement with the citizenry.

Economic Policy Reforms

Economic Policy Reforms

Economic Policy Reforms

The economic landscape of Planet Nebula has undergone significant transformations over the past few decades, driven by a combination of internal pressures and external influences. This section examines the major economic policy reforms that have shaped Nebulian society, focusing on the transition to market capitalism, the emergence of the green economy, and the implications of these changes on social equity and sustainability.

Transition to Market Capitalism

The shift towards market capitalism on Planet Nebula can be traced back to the late 21st century when the Nebulian government recognized the limitations of its previous state-controlled economic model. The decision to embrace market capitalism was influenced by several factors, including the need for increased efficiency, innovation, and competitiveness in a globalized economy.

The core tenets of market capitalism emphasize private ownership, voluntary exchange, and the role of supply and demand in determining prices. This framework can be mathematically represented by the fundamental equation of supply and demand:

$$P = f(Q_d, Q_s) \tag{16}$$

where P is the price of goods, Q_d is the quantity demanded, and Q_s is the quantity supplied.

As Nebula transitioned to this new economic paradigm, several key reforms were implemented:

+ **Privatization of State-Owned Enterprises:** The government initiated a widespread privatization program, selling off state-owned enterprises to private investors. This move aimed to improve efficiency and reduce the fiscal burden on the government. However, it also led to significant job losses and increased income inequality.

+ **Deregulation:** The Nebulian government began to roll back regulations that had previously stifled competition. This deregulation was intended to foster a more dynamic business environment. However, it also raised concerns about consumer protection and environmental sustainability.

+ **Tax Reforms:** A comprehensive tax reform was introduced to incentivize investment and stimulate economic growth. This included lowering corporate tax rates and simplifying the tax code. However, critics argued that these reforms disproportionately benefited the wealthy, exacerbating income inequality.

The impact of these economic policy reforms has been profound, leading to a surge in economic growth. However, the benefits have not been evenly distributed, resulting in significant disparities in wealth and opportunity across different segments of Nebulian society.

Impact on Income Inequality

One of the most pressing issues arising from the transition to market capitalism has been the widening gap between the rich and the poor. While the economy has expanded, the benefits of this growth have not been equitably shared.

The Gini coefficient, a common measure of income inequality, has shown a troubling upward trend in Nebula:

$$G = \frac{A}{A + B} \tag{17}$$

where G is the Gini coefficient, A represents the area between the line of perfect equality and the Lorenz curve, and B represents the area under the Lorenz curve. A Gini coefficient of 0 indicates perfect equality, while a coefficient of 1 indicates maximum inequality.

In Nebula, the Gini coefficient rose from 0.25 in the early 21st century to 0.45 by 2075, indicating a significant increase in income inequality. This disparity has sparked public outcry and calls for reforms aimed at wealth redistribution and social safety nets.

Debate Over Wealth Distribution and Social Safety Nets

The growing income inequality has prompted a robust debate regarding the role of government in wealth distribution and the necessity of social safety nets. Proponents of wealth redistribution argue that it is essential to ensure a fair and just society. They advocate for policies such as progressive taxation, universal basic income (UBI), and enhanced social services.

For example, the implementation of UBI has been proposed as a solution to combat poverty and provide a safety net for all citizens. The basic premise of UBI can be expressed mathematically as follows:

$$UBI = \frac{T}{N} \tag{18}$$

where UBI is the universal basic income per individual, T is the total tax revenue, and N is the number of citizens.

On the other hand, opponents of wealth redistribution contend that it may disincentivize hard work and innovation. They argue that a free-market system should be allowed to function without government interference, positing that economic growth will ultimately benefit all strata of society.

The debate continues, with policymakers grappling with the challenge of balancing economic growth with social equity. As Nebula moves forward, the outcomes of these economic policy reforms will play a crucial role in shaping the future of governance and societal well-being.

Conclusion

In conclusion, the economic policy reforms on Planet Nebula represent a significant shift towards market capitalism, characterized by privatization, deregulation, and tax reforms. While these changes have spurred economic growth, they have also led to increased income inequality and raised critical questions about wealth distribution and social safety nets. The ongoing debate surrounding these issues will undoubtedly influence the trajectory of Nebulian society in the years to come. As the planet navigates these complex challenges, it must strive to create an inclusive economic environment that promotes both prosperity and equity for all its citizens.

Embracing market capitalism

Privatization of key industries

Privatization refers to the process of transferring ownership of a public sector enterprise to private individuals or organizations. On Planet Nebula, the privatization of key industries has been a contentious issue, marked by significant economic, social, and political implications. This section will explore the theoretical underpinnings of privatization, the problems it has generated, and relevant examples from Nebula's experience.

Theoretical Foundations of Privatization

The theory of privatization is grounded in several economic principles, primarily those advocating for market efficiency and competition. Proponents argue that privatization leads to improved efficiency, innovation, and responsiveness to consumer needs. The fundamental theorem of welfare economics suggests that competitive markets can lead to Pareto efficiency, where resources are allocated in a way that maximizes total welfare.

Pareto Efficiency: A state where no individual can be made better off without making sor

$$(19)$$

Moreover, privatization is often justified through the lens of public choice theory, which posits that government entities are prone to inefficiencies due to lack of competition and the influence of special interest groups. By transferring ownership to the private sector, it is believed that firms will operate more efficiently due to profit motives and competitive pressures.

Key Industries Targeted for Privatization

In Nebula, several key industries have been targeted for privatization, including:

- **Energy Sector:** The state-owned Nebulian Energy Corporation (NEC) was privatized in 2030, with the intention of increasing competition and reducing energy prices.

- **Telecommunications:** The Nebulian Communications Authority (NCA) was privatized in 2025, leading to a surge in service providers and technological advancements.

- **Transportation:** The privatization of Nebula Railways aimed to enhance efficiency and service quality, though it faced significant public backlash.

Problems Arising from Privatization

Despite the theoretical benefits, the privatization of key industries in Nebula has encountered several problems:

- **Income Inequality:** Privatization has often led to increased income inequality, as wealth generated from privatized industries tends to concentrate among a small elite. For instance, the privatization of NEC resulted in significant profits for shareholders, while energy prices soared, disproportionately affecting lower-income households.

- **Job Losses:** The transition from public to private ownership often leads to job cuts as companies seek to maximize profits through cost-cutting measures. In 2031, following the privatization of Nebula Railways, thousands of workers faced layoffs, sparking widespread protests.

- **Quality of Services:** While competition is expected to improve service quality, many privatized sectors experienced a decline in service standards. The privatized telecommunications sector saw increased prices and reduced customer service quality, leading to public dissatisfaction.

Examples of Privatization Outcomes

The outcomes of privatization in Nebula provide a mixed picture.

- **Success in Telecommunications:** The privatization of NCA led to a rapid expansion of internet access and mobile services, with multiple providers competing for customers. This resulted in lower prices and improved technology, benefiting the populace.

- **Challenges in Energy:** In contrast, the privatization of NEC faced significant backlash due to rising energy costs. The government eventually had to intervene to regulate prices, highlighting the potential pitfalls of unchecked privatization.

- **Public Transport Struggles:** The privatization of Nebula Railways is often cited as a cautionary tale. While initial investments improved infrastructure, the focus on profitability led to reduced service frequency and increased ticket prices, alienating many commuters.

Conclusion

The privatization of key industries on Planet Nebula illustrates the complexities of transitioning from public to private ownership. While the theoretical benefits of efficiency and innovation are compelling, the real-world implications often reveal significant challenges, including increased inequality, job losses, and variable service quality. As Nebula continues to navigate these changes, it is essential to consider the lessons learned from past privatization efforts to inform future governance strategies.

In summary, the privatization of key industries can lead to both opportunities and challenges. Policymakers must balance the drive for efficiency with the need to protect vulnerable populations and ensure equitable access to essential services. The experiences of Nebula serve as a reminder that while privatization can be a tool for economic growth, it requires careful implementation and oversight to truly benefit society as a whole.

Impact on income inequality

The transition to market capitalism on Planet Nebula has had profound implications for income inequality. As the society embraced privatization of key industries, the economic landscape shifted dramatically, leading to both opportunities and challenges in wealth distribution. This section explores the multifaceted impact of these reforms on income inequality, drawing on relevant economic theories, statistical analyses, and real-world examples from Nebula's experience.

Theoretical Framework

To understand the impact of market capitalism on income inequality, we can reference the Kuznets Curve, which posits that as an economy develops, market forces first increase and then decrease economic inequality. The initial phase of economic growth often benefits those who are already wealthy, as they possess the capital necessary to invest in new opportunities. Over time, however, as the economy matures and social policies are implemented, income inequality may diminish.

The relationship can be expressed mathematically as:

$$I = f(GDP, P, S) \tag{20}$$

where I represents income inequality, GDP is the gross domestic product, P denotes population growth, and S signifies social policies aimed at wealth redistribution. This equation suggests that as GDP increases, income inequality may initially rise due to capital accumulation among the wealthy, but effective social policies can mitigate this effect.

Quantitative Analysis of Income Inequality

In the early years following the implementation of market capitalism, Nebula experienced a significant rise in income inequality. According to data from the Nebulian Bureau of Economic Statistics (NBES), the Gini coefficient—a common measure of income inequality—rose from 0.30 in the pre-capitalist era to 0.45 within a decade of privatization. This increase indicates a widening gap between the rich and the poor, with the top 10% of income earners capturing a disproportionate share of economic growth.

The data reveals that while the economy grew at an average rate of 5% per year, the wealth generated was not evenly distributed. The top income earners saw their incomes grow by 8% annually, whereas the bottom 50% experienced a mere 2% growth. This disparity can be attributed to several factors, including access to education, capital, and employment opportunities.

Case Studies of Income Disparities

One illustrative case is that of the Nebulian Tech Sector, which flourished post-privatization. Companies like NebulaTech and AstroDynamics attracted significant investment, leading to substantial profits. However, these gains were not shared equitably. For instance, while the average salary for tech workers surged to $120,000 annually, entry-level positions often paid less than $30,000, exacerbating income disparities.

Conversely, in the agricultural sector, which remained largely underfunded and subject to traditional practices, income stagnated. Farmers reported incomes below the poverty line, highlighting a stark contrast between sectors benefiting from globalization and those left behind. The following equation illustrates the disparity in income growth between sectors:

$$\Delta I_{sector} = I_{final} - I_{initial} = (I_{tech} - I_{agri}) \tag{21}$$

where ΔI_{sector} represents the change in income between the tech and agricultural sectors, I_{final} is the final income level, and $I_{initial}$ is the initial income level for each sector.

Public Response and Policy Implications

The growing income inequality sparked public outcry and led to the rise of grassroots movements advocating for social justice and economic reform. The Progressive Coalition, a political faction emerging from these movements, pushed for policies aimed at wealth redistribution, including higher taxes on the wealthy and increased funding for social programs.

In response, the government implemented a progressive tax system, which increased the tax rate for the top 5% of earners from 25% to 40%. This policy aimed to redistribute wealth more equitably across the population and was predicted to generate an additional $1 billion in revenue annually, which could be reinvested into education and healthcare.

Conclusion

The impact of market capitalism on income inequality on Planet Nebula has been profound and multifaceted. While economic growth has created opportunities for some, it has also led to significant disparities in wealth and income. The initial rise in inequality, as predicted by the Kuznets Curve, underscores the importance of implementing effective social policies to mitigate these effects. As Nebula continues to navigate its economic landscape, the lessons learned from these shifts will be crucial in shaping future governance and ensuring a more equitable society.

In summary, the transition to market capitalism has not only transformed the economy of Planet Nebula but has also highlighted the critical relationship between economic policies and income inequality. The ongoing challenge will be to balance growth with equity, ensuring that the benefits of prosperity are shared among all Nebulians.

Debate over wealth distribution and social safety nets

The debate over wealth distribution and social safety nets on Planet Nebula has intensified in recent decades, particularly following the rapid shift towards market capitalism. As the economy transitioned, the disparities in wealth became increasingly pronounced, leading to widespread discussions on the fairness and effectiveness of existing policies. This section explores the theoretical underpinnings of wealth distribution, the challenges it presents, and examples from Nebula's experience.

Theoretical Framework

Wealth distribution theories can be broadly categorized into two schools of thought: egalitarianism and utilitarianism.

Egalitarianism posits that all individuals should have equal access to resources and opportunities. This perspective is grounded in the belief that inequality can lead to social unrest and decreased overall societal welfare. The equation representing egalitarian wealth distribution can be expressed as:

$$W_i = \frac{W_{total}}{N} \tag{22}$$

where W_i is the wealth of each individual, W_{total} is the total wealth of the society, and N is the number of individuals. This model advocates for policies that ensure wealth is distributed equally among the population.

Utilitarianism , on the other hand, suggests that resources should be allocated in a manner that maximizes overall happiness, even if it results in unequal wealth distribution. The utilitarian approach can be summarized by the equation:

$$U = \sum_{i=1}^{N} U(W_i) \tag{23}$$

where U represents total utility, and $U(W_i)$ is the utility derived from the wealth of individual i. This perspective supports the idea that some degree of inequality may be acceptable if it contributes to a greater total utility.

Challenges in Wealth Distribution

The debate surrounding wealth distribution on Planet Nebula is fraught with challenges. One major issue is the increasing income inequality, which has been exacerbated by the privatization of key industries. The Gini coefficient, a measure of income inequality, has shown a marked increase, indicating a widening gap between the wealthy elite and the lower-income population.

$$G = \frac{A}{A + B} \tag{24}$$

where G is the Gini coefficient, A represents the area between the line of equality and the Lorenz curve, and B is the area under the Lorenz curve. A Gini coefficient of 0 represents perfect equality, while a coefficient of 1 indicates extreme inequality. Nebula's Gini coefficient has risen to 0.45, signifying a significant imbalance in wealth distribution.

Another challenge is the perception of social safety nets. While proponents argue that safety nets are essential for protecting the most vulnerable members of society, critics claim they create dependency and disincentivize work. This debate is compounded by the increasing costs associated with welfare programs, leading to calls for reform and reevaluation of existing policies.

Examples from Nebula

The implementation of the Universal Basic Income (UBI) program on Planet Nebula serves as a notable example of a wealth distribution strategy. Initiated as an experiment in the capital city of Nebulopolis, UBI aimed to provide all citizens with a monthly stipend, regardless of their employment status. Proponents argued that this would reduce poverty and stimulate the economy by increasing consumer spending.

However, the UBI program faced significant challenges. Initial findings indicated that while some residents reported improved quality of life, others used the funds to support non-productive habits, leading to debates over the program's long-term sustainability. The economic implications of UBI are encapsulated by the following equation:

$$GDP_{new} = C + I + G + (X - M) \tag{25}$$

where GDP_{new} is the new Gross Domestic Product, C is consumer spending, I is investment, G is government spending, X is exports, and M is imports. The effectiveness of UBI in stimulating C was a critical factor in evaluating its success.

In contrast, the introduction of a progressive taxation system aimed at redistributing wealth has also been a focal point of the debate. This system imposes higher tax rates on the wealthiest citizens, with the intention of funding social safety nets and public services. The effectiveness of this system can be analyzed through the following tax revenue equation:

$$TR = \sum_{i=1}^{N} T_i \cdot W_i \tag{26}$$

where TR represents total tax revenue, T_i is the tax rate for individual i, and W_i is the wealth of individual i. Critics of the progressive tax system argue that it may discourage investment and innovation, leading to a potential slowdown in economic growth.

Conclusion

The debate over wealth distribution and social safety nets on Planet Nebula illustrates the complexities inherent in governance and economic policy. While efforts to address income inequality through programs like UBI and progressive taxation have been implemented, the challenges of dependency, sustainability, and economic impact remain contentious. As Nebula continues to navigate these issues, it is crucial for policymakers to consider the diverse perspectives and potential long-term implications of their decisions on wealth distribution and social safety nets. Ultimately, the success of these policies will depend on their ability to balance equity and efficiency, ensuring that all citizens have the opportunity to thrive in a rapidly changing economic landscape.

The Green Economy

Transition to renewable energy sources

The transition to renewable energy sources on Planet Nebula represents a pivotal shift in the governance and economic policy framework of the society. This section explores the theoretical underpinnings of renewable energy, the challenges faced during the transition, and notable examples that illustrate both successes and setbacks in this endeavor.

Theoretical Framework

The transition to renewable energy is grounded in several theoretical perspectives, including ecological modernization theory, which posits that environmental sustainability can be achieved through technological innovation and economic growth. This theory suggests that by investing in renewable energy technologies, societies can decouple economic growth from environmental degradation, thus promoting a sustainable future.

Mathematically, the potential of renewable energy can be represented by the following equation:

$$E_{renewable} = \sum_{i=1}^{n} P_i \cdot T_i \tag{27}$$

where $E_{renewable}$ is the total energy output from renewable sources, P_i is the power output of each renewable technology (e.g., solar, wind, hydro), and T_i is the time duration for which that power output is generated.

This equation underscores the importance of diversifying energy sources to maximize output and ensure energy security. The diversification of energy sources is critical for mitigating the risks associated with reliance on a single type of energy, such as fossil fuels, which are subject to market volatility and geopolitical tensions.

Challenges in Transitioning

Despite the theoretical advantages of renewable energy, the transition on Planet Nebula has not been without its challenges:

- **Infrastructure Limitations:** Many regions on Nebula lack the necessary infrastructure to support large-scale renewable energy projects. For instance, rural areas often face challenges in connecting to the national grid, which hampers the deployment of solar and wind farms.

- **Economic Barriers:** The initial capital investment required for renewable energy technologies can be prohibitively high. This economic barrier is particularly pronounced in developing regions where funding and investment are limited.

- **Public Resistance:** There is often public skepticism regarding the effectiveness and reliability of renewable energy sources. Historical reliance on fossil fuels has created a cultural inertia that resists change, as seen in the protests against wind farms in Nebula's coastal regions.

- **Policy Inconsistencies:** Fluctuations in government policy can lead to uncertainty in the renewable energy sector. For instance, changes in subsidies for solar energy have caused confusion and disrupted investment flows, leading to stalled projects and lost opportunities.

Examples of Success and Setbacks

Several initiatives have demonstrated both the potential and the challenges of transitioning to renewable energy on Planet Nebula:

Successes   1. **Solar Energy Initiatives in the Desert Regions:** The Nebulian government launched an ambitious solar energy project in the vast desert regions, which has successfully harnessed the abundant sunlight. The project, known as the Solar Nexus, has increased the share of solar energy in the national grid from 5% to 25% in just five years. This initiative has not only reduced carbon emissions but has also created thousands of jobs in the region.

2. Wind Farms along the Coastal Areas: The establishment of offshore wind farms has proven to be a game-changer for Nebula's energy landscape. These wind farms have the capacity to generate up to 40% of the country's electricity needs, significantly reducing reliance on fossil fuels. The success of these projects has encouraged further investment in renewable technologies, demonstrating a positive feedback loop in policy and public support.

Setbacks 1. Hydroelectric Projects and Environmental Concerns: While hydroelectric power is a significant renewable energy source, the construction of dams has led to ecological disruptions. The River Zeta Dam project faced backlash from environmental groups due to its impact on local wildlife and indigenous communities. This situation highlights the need for a balanced approach that considers ecological and social factors in energy policy.

2. Battery Storage Issues: The reliance on intermittent energy sources such as solar and wind has raised concerns about energy storage capabilities. The Nebulian government invested heavily in battery storage technology, yet technical issues and high costs have limited the effectiveness of these investments. As a result, energy reliability remains a critical challenge for the renewable sector.

Conclusion

The transition to renewable energy sources on Planet Nebula is a complex and multifaceted process. While the theoretical benefits of renewable energy are clear, the practical challenges require careful navigation through infrastructure, economic, public, and policy-related hurdles. Successful examples, such as the Solar Nexus and offshore wind farms, provide valuable lessons, while setbacks underscore the importance of a holistic approach to energy governance. As Nebula continues on this path, the integration of renewable energy will not only reshape its energy landscape but will also serve as a model for other societies grappling with similar transitions.

Sustainable development policies

Sustainable development policies are essential for ensuring that the needs of the present are met without compromising the ability of future generations to meet their own needs. This concept, rooted in the Brundtland Report of 1987, emphasizes the interconnectedness of economic growth, environmental stewardship, and social equity. On Planet Nebula, the implementation of sustainable development policies has been a response to the pressing challenges of resource depletion, environmental degradation, and social inequality.

Theoretical Framework

The theoretical framework for sustainable development policies on Planet Nebula draws from various disciplines, including economics, environmental science, and sociology. Key theories include:

1. **Ecological Economics**: This theory integrates ecological and economic principles, advocating for the valuation of natural capital and ecosystem services. It emphasizes that economic activities must stay within the planet's ecological limits to avoid environmental collapse.

2. **Social Justice Theory**: This approach highlights the importance of equity in the distribution of resources and opportunities. Sustainable development must address the needs of marginalized populations, ensuring that all Nebulians have access to essential services and resources.

3. **Systems Theory**: This perspective views the economy, society, and environment as interconnected systems. Policies must consider the feedback loops and interactions among these systems to create holistic solutions.

Challenges in Implementation

Despite the theoretical underpinnings, the implementation of sustainable development policies on Planet Nebula faces several challenges:

1. **Resource Conflicts**: Competition for limited resources often leads to conflicts among different sectors, such as agriculture, industry, and conservation. Balancing these interests requires effective negotiation and conflict resolution mechanisms.

2. **Economic Pressures**: The push for short-term economic growth can undermine long-term sustainability goals. Policymakers often prioritize immediate economic benefits over sustainable practices, leading to environmental degradation.

3. **Public Awareness and Engagement**: A lack of public understanding of sustainable development principles can hinder policy implementation. Engaging citizens in decision-making processes is crucial for fostering a culture of sustainability.

4. **Technological Limitations**: While technology can provide solutions for sustainable development, there are limitations in terms of accessibility, affordability, and scalability of green technologies.

Examples of Sustainable Development Policies

On Planet Nebula, several innovative policies have been implemented to promote sustainable development:

1. **Renewable Energy Initiatives**: The Nebulian government has invested heavily in renewable energy sources, including solar, wind, and hydroelectric power. By 2030, the aim is to achieve a 70% reliance on renewable energy, significantly reducing greenhouse gas emissions. The equation governing energy transition can be expressed as:

$$E_{renewable} = E_{total} \times R$$

where $E_{renewable}$ is the amount of energy generated from renewable sources, E_{total} is the total energy consumption, and R is the percentage of renewable energy targeted.

2. **Sustainable Agriculture Practices**: The introduction of agroecological practices has been pivotal in reducing the environmental impact of agriculture. Policies encouraging crop rotation, organic farming, and integrated pest management have led to increased biodiversity and soil health.

3. **Urban Sustainability Programs**: Nebulian cities have adopted smart growth principles, promoting compact urban development, public transportation, and green spaces. The emphasis is on reducing urban sprawl and enhancing the quality of life for residents.

4. **Waste Management Policies**: The implementation of a circular economy model encourages recycling and reusing materials to minimize waste. Policies mandating waste separation and composting have led to a significant reduction in landfill use.

Policy Evaluation and Impact Assessment

To ensure the effectiveness of sustainable development policies, regular evaluation and impact assessment are essential. The following indicators are used to measure progress:

1. **Environmental Indicators**: Metrics such as carbon emissions, biodiversity levels, and water quality are monitored to assess the environmental impact of policies.

2. **Social Indicators**: Assessing access to education, healthcare, and basic services helps evaluate the social equity aspect of sustainable development.

3. **Economic Indicators**: Economic growth rates, employment levels in green sectors, and income distribution are analyzed to measure the economic viability of sustainable practices.

The evaluation process can be represented by the equation:

$$S = \frac{E + S + E}{3}$$

where S is the sustainability score, E represents environmental indicators, S stands for social indicators, and E indicates economic indicators.

Conclusion

Sustainable development policies on Planet Nebula are critical for addressing the multifaceted challenges of the 21st century. By integrating economic, social, and environmental considerations, Nebulian governance aims to create a resilient society capable of thriving in harmony with its environment. The ongoing evaluation and adaptation of these policies will be essential to navigate the complexities of sustainability in an ever-changing world.

Economic impacts and job creation

The transition to a green economy on Planet Nebula has not only redefined the environmental landscape but has also significantly impacted economic structures and job creation strategies. This section explores the economic ramifications of this transition, highlighting both opportunities and challenges that have emerged.

Theoretical Framework

The economic impacts of transitioning to a green economy can be analyzed through the lens of the *Green Growth Theory*. This theory posits that economic growth and environmental sustainability are not mutually exclusive but can be pursued simultaneously. Key components of this theory include:

- **Sustainable Development:** This principle emphasizes the need to meet the needs of the present without compromising the ability of future generations to meet their own needs.

- **Decoupling:** The process of reducing the environmental impact of economic growth, often measured as the decoupling of GDP growth from greenhouse gas emissions.

- **Innovation and Technology:** The role of technological advancements in creating new markets and job opportunities while reducing environmental footprints.

The equation representing the relationship between economic growth (EG), environmental sustainability (ES), and employment (E) can be expressed as:

$$EG = f(ES, E) \tag{28}$$

where f is a function that illustrates how economic growth is dependent on both environmental sustainability and employment levels.

Job Creation in the Green Economy

The shift towards renewable energy sources and sustainable practices has created a plethora of job opportunities across various sectors. According to recent studies, the green economy has the potential to generate millions of jobs in sectors such as renewable energy, energy efficiency, waste management, and sustainable agriculture.

1. Renewable Energy Sector The renewable energy sector is a primary driver of job creation on Planet Nebula. As the government invests heavily in solar, wind, and hydroelectric power, it has led to the establishment of numerous manufacturing plants and service providers. For example, the construction of solar farms has resulted in the creation of jobs in:

- **Manufacturing:** Production of solar panels and wind turbines.

- **Installation:** Skilled labor for the installation of renewable energy systems.

- **Maintenance:** Ongoing maintenance services for renewable energy facilities.

The growth in this sector has been substantial, with estimates suggesting that for every megawatt of solar energy installed, approximately 5.65 jobs are created [?].

2. Energy Efficiency Initiatives Energy efficiency initiatives have also contributed to job creation. Programs aimed at retrofitting buildings, improving insulation, and upgrading heating and cooling systems have increased demand for skilled labor. The *Energy Efficiency Jobs Report* indicates that investments in energy efficiency can yield up to 2.5 million jobs annually on Planet Nebula [?].

3. Sustainable Agriculture   The agricultural sector has seen a transformation towards sustainable practices, which has led to job creation in areas such as organic farming, agroecology, and local food systems. The shift to sustainable agriculture not only enhances food security but also provides employment opportunities in rural areas, contributing to local economies.

Challenges and Problems

Despite the positive impacts of transitioning to a green economy, several challenges persist that could hinder job creation:

1. Skill Gaps   A significant challenge is the skill gap in the labor market. Many workers in traditional industries may lack the necessary skills to transition to green jobs. This necessitates comprehensive training programs to equip the workforce with relevant skills. The government must invest in educational initiatives that focus on renewable energy technologies and sustainable practices.

2. Economic Displacement   The transition to a green economy may lead to economic displacement for workers in fossil fuel industries. As these industries decline, it is crucial to implement policies that support affected workers through retraining programs and social safety nets.

3. Funding and Investment   The success of job creation in the green economy is contingent upon adequate funding and investment. The government of Planet Nebula must prioritize investments in green technologies and infrastructure to sustain job growth. Public-private partnerships can play a critical role in mobilizing resources for green initiatives.

Examples of Successful Initiatives

Several successful initiatives on Planet Nebula demonstrate the potential for job creation in the green economy:

- **Nebula Solar Initiative:** A government-backed program that incentivizes solar panel installation in residential areas, resulting in the creation of over 50,000 jobs in the last five years.

- **Green Building Standards:** Implementation of stringent green building standards has led to the retrofitting of thousands of buildings, creating jobs in construction and energy auditing.

- **Community Farming Programs:** Local governments have supported community farming initiatives, providing jobs in urban agriculture and promoting food sovereignty.

Conclusion

The transition to a green economy on Planet Nebula presents both opportunities and challenges for job creation. While the shift towards renewable energy, energy efficiency, and sustainable practices has the potential to generate substantial employment, addressing skill gaps, economic displacement, and funding challenges is crucial for maximizing these benefits. By investing in education, supporting displaced workers, and fostering public-private partnerships, Planet Nebula can pave the way for a sustainable and prosperous future.

Trade and Foreign Policy

Globalization and Free Trade Agreements

Globalization, defined as the increasing interconnectedness of economies, cultures, and populations across the globe, has played a pivotal role in shaping the economic landscape of Planet Nebula. This phenomenon is characterized by the expansion of international trade, investment, and the flow of information. Free trade agreements (FTAs) serve as a crucial mechanism in this process, aiming to reduce or eliminate barriers to trade between participating nations.

Theoretical Framework

The underlying theory of free trade is rooted in classical economics, particularly the principle of comparative advantage. This principle posits that countries should specialize in the production of goods and services they can produce most efficiently, thereby maximizing overall economic welfare. The equation that captures this concept is:

$$\text{Total Output} = \sum_{i=1}^{n} \text{Output}_i \tag{29}$$

where Output_i represents the output of country i in the production of goods where it holds a comparative advantage.

Additionally, the Heckscher-Ohlin model expands on this by suggesting that countries will export goods that utilize their abundant factors of production while importing goods that require factors in which they are scarce. This model can be represented as:

$$Exports = f(\text{Factor Abundance, Goods}) \qquad (30)$$

Benefits of Free Trade Agreements

Free trade agreements on Planet Nebula have led to several economic benefits:

+ **Increased Market Access:** FTAs allow Nebulian businesses to access larger markets without the burden of tariffs and quotas, enabling them to scale operations and increase profitability.

+ **Enhanced Competition:** By reducing trade barriers, FTAs foster competition, leading to lower prices and improved quality of goods and services for consumers.

+ **Foreign Direct Investment (FDI):** FTAs often attract foreign investments, as they signal a commitment to open markets and stable economic policies, further stimulating economic growth.

+ **Innovation and Technology Transfer:** With the influx of foreign companies and partnerships, Nebulian firms benefit from the transfer of technology and innovative practices, enhancing productivity.

Challenges and Criticisms

Despite the potential benefits, globalization and FTAs have also faced significant challenges and criticisms:

+ **Income Inequality:** The benefits of FTAs are often unevenly distributed, leading to increased income inequality within Nebula. Regions or sectors that are less competitive may suffer job losses, while others thrive.

+ **Loss of Sovereignty:** Critics argue that FTAs can undermine national sovereignty, as domestic policies may be influenced or constrained by international agreements.

+ **Environmental Concerns:** Increased production and trade can lead to environmental degradation, as companies may exploit resources without adequate regulatory oversight. This raises questions about sustainable practices in a globalized economy.

+ **Cultural Homogenization:** The spread of global trade can lead to the erosion of local cultures and traditions, as global brands and products overshadow local enterprises.

Examples from Planet Nebula

Several key FTAs have been established on Planet Nebula, impacting its economic landscape:

+ **The Nebula Trade Pact (NTP):** Signed between the central government and neighboring regions, the NTP aimed to eliminate tariffs on 80% of goods within five years. Early analysis indicated a 15% increase in trade volume, but also highlighted significant job losses in the textile sector, raising concerns about the agreement's overall impact.

+ **The Intergalactic Trade Agreement (ITA):** This ambitious FTA expanded trade relations beyond Nebula, including other planets in the system. While it facilitated new markets for Nebulian tech companies, it also faced backlash from local farmers who struggled to compete with imported agricultural products.

Conclusion

In conclusion, globalization and free trade agreements have profoundly influenced the economic policies of Planet Nebula. While these agreements offer substantial opportunities for growth and development, they also pose significant challenges that require careful management and policy consideration. As Nebula continues to navigate the complexities of globalization, it is imperative to address the disparities and environmental impacts associated with these economic shifts to ensure a sustainable and equitable future.

Bibliography

[1] Adam Smith, *The Wealth of Nations*, 1776.

[2] David Ricardo, *On the Principles of Political Economy and Taxation*, 1817.

[3] Paul Krugman, *Geography and Trade*, 1991.

[4] Joseph Stiglitz, *Globalization and Its Discontents*, 2002.

Protectionism and Economic Nationalism

The concept of protectionism refers to the economic policy of restricting imports from other countries through methods such as tariffs, quotas, and other trade barriers. Economic nationalism, on the other hand, emphasizes domestic control of the economy, prioritizing national interests over international considerations. This section explores the implications of protectionism and economic nationalism on Planet Nebula, examining the theoretical underpinnings, associated problems, and real-world examples from Nebulian society.

Theoretical Framework

Protectionism is grounded in several economic theories, notably the Infant Industry Argument and the Strategic Trade Theory. The Infant Industry Argument posits that emerging industries may require temporary protection from foreign competition to develop and become competitive. This theory is often used to justify tariffs and subsidies aimed at nurturing local businesses.

$$\text{Tariff Revenue} = \text{Tariff Rate} \times \text{Quantity of Imports} \qquad (31)$$

Strategic Trade Theory suggests that government intervention can enhance the competitive position of domestic firms in global markets. By protecting key industries, governments can create a favorable environment for innovation and growth, which can lead to increased national income.

However, protectionism often comes with significant drawbacks. Economists argue that it can lead to inefficiencies, higher prices for consumers, and retaliatory measures from other nations. The following sections will delve into these issues as they pertain to Nebula.

Problems Associated with Protectionism

1. **Increased Prices**: One of the most immediate effects of protectionist policies is the increase in prices for consumers. Tariffs raise the cost of imported goods, leading to higher prices in the domestic market. For example, following the implementation of tariffs on imported textiles, Nebulian consumers saw an average price increase of 25% for clothing items, disproportionately affecting lower-income households.

2. **Inefficiencies and Resource Misallocation**: Protectionism can lead to inefficiencies in the economy by supporting industries that may not be viable without government assistance. This misallocation of resources can stifle innovation and reduce overall productivity. For instance, Nebula's automobile industry, heavily subsidized and protected from foreign competition, has struggled to innovate compared to its global counterparts, resulting in a stagnant market.

3. **Retaliation and Trade Wars**: Protectionist measures often provoke retaliation from trading partners, leading to trade wars. Nebula's recent imposition of tariffs on agricultural products prompted a swift response from neighboring planets, resulting in a cycle of escalating tariffs that harmed Nebulian exporters.

4. **Impact on Global Supply Chains**: In an increasingly interconnected world, protectionism can disrupt global supply chains. Nebulian manufacturers relying on imported components faced delays and increased costs, leading to production slowdowns. The disruption of the supply chain for electronic components, crucial for Nebula's tech industry, exemplified this issue.

Examples from Planet Nebula

The Nebulian government has implemented various protectionist policies in recent years, particularly in response to economic challenges. One notable example is the imposition of tariffs on imported agricultural products to protect local farmers. While this policy aimed to bolster domestic agriculture, it resulted in higher food prices and strained relations with agricultural-exporting planets.

Another example is the establishment of quotas on foreign steel imports. This measure was intended to protect Nebula's steel industry from foreign competition. However, the unintended consequence was a significant increase in construction costs, as local builders faced higher prices for steel, ultimately impacting housing affordability.

Economic Nationalism in Nebula

Economic nationalism has gained traction in Nebula as citizens increasingly prioritize local over global interests. This shift has manifested in calls for policies that favor domestic industries and workers. The rise of the "Buy Nebulian" movement, which encourages consumers to purchase locally-made products, reflects this sentiment.

While economic nationalism can foster a sense of pride and community, it also raises concerns about isolationism and the potential for reduced international cooperation. Nebula's withdrawal from several trade agreements has sparked debates about the long-term implications for economic growth and global partnerships.

Conclusion

In conclusion, protectionism and economic nationalism present a complex array of challenges and opportunities for Planet Nebula. While these policies can provide short-term relief for domestic industries, they often lead to higher consumer prices, inefficiencies, and strained international relations. As Nebula navigates its economic future, policymakers must carefully weigh the benefits of protectionism against its potential drawbacks, ensuring that the pursuit of national interests does not come at the expense of long-term economic health and global cooperation.

Balancing National Interests with Global Cooperation

In an increasingly interconnected world, the challenge of balancing national interests with global cooperation has become paramount for the governance of Planet Nebula. This balance is not merely an ethical consideration; it is a strategic necessity that impacts economic stability, social cohesion, and environmental sustainability.

Theoretical Framework

The theoretical underpinning of this balance can be understood through the lens of International Relations (IR) theories, particularly Realism and Liberalism.

Realism posits that states act primarily in their own self-interest, prioritizing national security and economic prosperity over cooperative efforts. In contrast, Liberalism advocates for international cooperation, emphasizing the importance of institutions and interdependence among states.

The equation that often summarizes this dynamic can be expressed as:

$$C = f(NI, GC) \tag{32}$$

where C represents the level of cooperation, NI denotes national interests, and GC signifies global cooperation efforts. The function f illustrates that the degree of cooperation is a function of the interplay between these two variables.

Challenges in Balancing Interests

The pursuit of national interests can lead to protectionist policies that undermine global cooperation. For instance, Nebula's recent shift towards economic nationalism has seen the rise of tariffs on imported goods, ostensibly to protect local industries. While this may bolster short-term economic gains for specific sectors, it risks retaliatory measures from trading partners, leading to a spiral of trade wars that can destabilize the economy.

Moreover, the environmental policies of Planet Nebula have been a contentious area. The commitment to reducing carbon emissions often clashes with the immediate economic interests of fossil fuel industries. The equation governing this tension can be expressed as:

$$E = NI - GC \tag{33}$$

where E represents environmental sustainability, NI is the pursuit of national economic interests, and GC is the commitment to global environmental agreements. This equation illustrates that an overemphasis on national interests can lead to environmental degradation, which ultimately undermines long-term national security.

Examples of Balancing Acts

One notable example of balancing national interests with global cooperation on Planet Nebula is the Nebulian Climate Accord. This agreement was established to commit member states to specific emissions reduction targets while allowing for flexibility in how these targets are met. The Accord has fostered cooperation among nations, exemplifying the potential for mutual benefit when national interests align with global goals.

Another instance is the Nebulian Trade Partnership, which aims to facilitate trade while ensuring that labor and environmental standards are upheld. By integrating these standards into trade agreements, Nebula has managed to protect its domestic industries while also engaging in beneficial global trade. The equation governing this partnership can be described as:

$$TP = NI + GC - C \qquad (34)$$

where TP stands for trade partnership effectiveness, NI represents national interests, GC denotes global cooperation, and C is the cost of compliance with international standards. This equation highlights that effective trade partnerships can be achieved when both national and global interests are considered.

Policy Recommendations

To enhance the balance between national interests and global cooperation, several policy recommendations can be made:

- **Incentivize Green Technologies:** The Nebulian government should provide subsidies and tax breaks for industries transitioning to renewable energy. This aligns national economic interests with global environmental goals.

- **Strengthen Multilateral Institutions:** Engaging in and supporting international organizations can help Nebula navigate complex global challenges while safeguarding its national interests.

- **Promote Public Awareness:** Educating citizens about the benefits of global cooperation can foster a culture of understanding and support for policies that may initially seem contrary to national interests.

Conclusion

In conclusion, the balancing act between national interests and global cooperation is not only a theoretical challenge but a practical necessity for Planet Nebula. By recognizing the interconnectedness of these two spheres, Nebula can pursue policies that promote both national prosperity and global stability. As Nebula navigates the complexities of governance in a globalized world, the lessons learned from this balance will be critical in shaping a sustainable and equitable future.

Social Policy Reforms

Social Policy Reforms

Social Policy Reforms

Social policy reforms on Planet Nebula have been a critical component of the governance evolution, reflecting the society's response to the dynamic needs of its citizens. These reforms aim to address issues of inequality, access to essential services, and the overall well-being of the population. The theoretical framework guiding these reforms is rooted in the principles of social justice, equity, and the welfare state, which advocate for a balanced approach to resource distribution and the provision of public goods.

Theoretical Framework

The theoretical underpinning of social policy reforms in Nebula can be traced to the social contract theory, which posits that individuals consent, either explicitly or implicitly, to surrender some freedoms to a governing body in exchange for protection of their remaining rights. This theory emphasizes the role of the state in ensuring social welfare and addressing disparities among its citizens.

$$\text{Social Welfare} = \frac{\text{Utility of Individual A} + \text{Utility of Individual B} + \ldots + \text{Utility of Indivi}}{N}$$

(35)

Where N is the total number of individuals in society. This equation illustrates that social welfare is maximized when the utilities of all individuals are taken into account, necessitating a comprehensive approach to policy-making.

Key Areas of Reform

The Nebulian government has identified several key areas for social policy reforms, including education, healthcare, and social justice initiatives.

Education and Skills Development   One of the most pressing areas for reform has been the education system. Historically, access to quality education has been uneven, with marginalized communities facing significant barriers. The government has implemented a series of reforms aimed at:

- Reforming the curriculum to include critical thinking and technological skills,

- Expanding access to quality education through scholarships and funding for under-resourced schools,

- Promoting vocational training and lifelong learning initiatives to equip citizens with relevant skills for the evolving job market.

These reforms are underpinned by the theory of human capital, which suggests that investments in education lead to higher productivity and economic growth. The government has allocated a significant portion of its budget to educational reforms, resulting in a measurable increase in literacy rates and employment outcomes.

Healthcare System Overhaul   Healthcare has emerged as another focal point for social policy reforms. The Nebulian healthcare system has historically been fragmented, leading to disparities in access and quality of care. In response, the government has embarked on a comprehensive healthcare overhaul, which includes:

- Implementing universal healthcare coverage to ensure that all citizens have access to necessary medical services,

- Establishing public-private partnerships to enhance service delivery and efficiency,

- Addressing healthcare disparities through targeted programs for vulnerable populations.

The economic theory of externalities is relevant here, as public health improvements can lead to broader societal benefits, such as increased productivity and reduced healthcare costs. The success of these reforms can be measured through key performance indicators such as life expectancy and patient satisfaction rates.

Social Justice Initiatives   Social justice initiatives have gained momentum in Nebula, focusing on equal rights and anti-discrimination laws. These initiatives are grounded in the principles of equity and inclusivity, aiming to dismantle systemic barriers faced by marginalized groups. Key components of these initiatives include:

- Enacting legislation to protect against discrimination based on gender, race, and sexual orientation,

- Promoting gender equality and women's empowerment through targeted programs and funding,

- Encouraging racial and ethnic diversity inclusion in public and private sectors.

The theory of intersectionality is particularly pertinent in this context, as it recognizes that individuals may face multiple, overlapping forms of discrimination. The government has established monitoring bodies to ensure compliance with social justice laws and to evaluate the effectiveness of these initiatives.

Challenges and Criticisms

Despite the progress made, social policy reforms in Nebula have faced significant challenges. Critics argue that:

- The pace of reform has been slow, with many initiatives failing to reach the most disadvantaged populations,

- There is a lack of adequate funding and resources to implement reforms effectively,

- Political resistance from traditionalist factions has hindered the advancement of progressive policies.

Public opinion has also played a role in shaping the discourse around social policy reforms. While many citizens support the need for change, there is skepticism regarding the government's ability to deliver on its promises. Opinion polls indicate that trust in political leaders and institutions has waned, which poses a challenge for the successful implementation of social policies.

Conclusion

In conclusion, social policy reforms on Planet Nebula represent a critical effort to address the diverse needs of its citizens and promote social equity. By focusing on education, healthcare, and social justice, the Nebulian government seeks to create a more inclusive society.   However, ongoing challenges and public skepticism necessitate continued efforts to engage citizens and ensure that reforms translate into tangible benefits for all.   The lessons learned from Nebula's social policy reforms may offer valuable insights for other societies grappling with similar issues of inequality and access to essential services.

Education and Skills Development

Reforming the education system

The education system on Planet Nebula has undergone significant transformations over the years, reflecting the changing socio-political landscape and the demands of a modern economy.   The reforming of the education system is not merely an administrative task;   it is a complex interplay of pedagogical theories, socio-economic factors, and cultural considerations. This section delves into the theoretical frameworks underpinning education reform, the challenges faced, and practical examples of successful initiatives.

Theoretical Frameworks

At the heart of educational reform are several key theories that guide policymakers and educators. Constructivist theory, championed by theorists such as Piaget and Vygotsky, posits that learners construct knowledge through experiences and interactions. This theory advocates for a student-centered approach, emphasizing critical thinking and problem-solving over rote memorization.

Moreover, the Human Capital Theory, articulated by economists like Becker, suggests that education is an investment in human capital, leading to increased productivity and economic growth. This theory underpins many reforms aimed at aligning educational outcomes with labor market needs, thereby fostering a more skilled workforce.

Challenges in Reforming the Education System

Despite the theoretical underpinnings, the reform of the education system on Planet Nebula faces several formidable challenges:

+ **Inequality in Access:** Disparities in access to quality education persist, particularly between urban and rural areas. According to a 2022 report by the Nebulian Education Ministry, students in rural regions are 30% less likely to have access to advanced placement courses compared to their urban counterparts.

+ **Curriculum Relevance:** The existing curriculum often fails to meet the needs of a rapidly changing economy. For instance, a 2021 survey indicated that 65% of Nebulian employers found graduates lacking in critical skills such as digital literacy and teamwork.

+ **Teacher Training and Retention:** Educators are the backbone of any reform, yet many face inadequate training and support. A staggering 40% of teachers reported feeling unprepared to teach the new curriculum introduced in 2020, leading to high turnover rates.

+ **Resistance to Change:** Cultural resistance to new educational paradigms can hinder reform efforts. Many stakeholders, including parents and community leaders, may be skeptical of changes that deviate from traditional educational practices.

Successful Initiatives

Despite these challenges, several successful initiatives have emerged in Nebula that serve as models for reform:

+ **Integrated STEM Programs:** In 2023, the Nebulian government launched a nationwide initiative to integrate Science, Technology, Engineering, and Mathematics (STEM) into the curriculum. Schools that adopted this approach reported a 25% increase in student engagement and a 15% rise in standardized test scores in these subjects.

+ **Community-Based Learning:** Programs that involve local communities in the educational process have gained traction. For example, the "Learn and Earn" initiative allows students to work with local businesses, providing them with practical experience while enhancing their learning. This program has seen a 20% increase in students pursuing careers in entrepreneurship.

+ **Digital Learning Platforms:** The introduction of digital learning platforms has revolutionized access to education. The Nebulian Education Network (NEN) allows students from remote areas to access high-quality educational resources and virtual classrooms. In 2022, NEN reported over 1 million active users, significantly bridging the educational gap.

* **Focus on Mental Health:** Recognizing the importance of mental well-being, schools have begun to incorporate mental health education into their curricula. Programs aimed at reducing stigma and providing support have led to a 30% decrease in reported mental health issues among students.

Conclusion

Reforming the education system on Planet Nebula is a multifaceted endeavor that requires a nuanced understanding of the interplay between theory and practice. While challenges such as inequality, curriculum relevance, and resistance to change persist, successful initiatives demonstrate that progress is possible. As Nebula continues to evolve, a commitment to innovative educational practices will be essential in preparing future generations for the complexities of an ever-changing world.

In summary, the path to educational reform on Planet Nebula is littered with obstacles, yet it is also rich with opportunities for growth and improvement. By embracing a holistic approach to education that prioritizes equity, relevance, and community involvement, Nebula can cultivate a generation of learners equipped to thrive in a dynamic and interconnected universe.

Access to quality education

Access to quality education is a fundamental pillar for the development of any society, including the diverse communities on Planet Nebula. It is not merely about the availability of schools or educational resources, but rather the equitable distribution of quality educational opportunities that enable individuals to reach their full potential. This section explores the theoretical frameworks surrounding access to education, identifies the challenges faced by Nebulian society, and provides examples of initiatives aimed at improving educational access.

Theoretical Frameworks

The concept of access to education can be examined through several theoretical lenses, including Human Capital Theory and Social Justice Theory.

Human Capital Theory posits that education is an investment in human capital, leading to increased productivity and economic growth. According to Becker

(1964), individuals who acquire higher levels of education typically enjoy better job prospects and higher wages. The relationship can be expressed as:

$$Y = f(H) \quad \text{where } Y \text{ is income and } H \text{ is human capital} \qquad (36)$$

This theory suggests that enhancing access to quality education can lead to a more skilled workforce, thereby fostering economic development on Planet Nebula.

Social Justice Theory, on the other hand, emphasizes equity and fairness in educational access. It argues that all individuals, regardless of their socio-economic background, should have the opportunity to receive a quality education. This perspective is particularly relevant in addressing the disparities observed in Nebulian society, where access to education is often influenced by factors such as income, geography, and ethnicity.

Challenges to Access

Despite the theoretical understanding of the importance of education, several challenges hinder access to quality education on Planet Nebula:

+ **Geographical Barriers:** Many rural areas on Nebula lack adequate educational facilities. Students in remote regions often face long travel distances to reach schools, which can deter attendance and participation.

+ **Economic Disparities:** Socio-economic status significantly impacts educational access. Families with limited financial resources may struggle to afford school fees, uniforms, and educational materials, leading to lower enrollment rates among disadvantaged groups.

+ **Cultural Factors:** In some Nebulian communities, cultural norms and values may prioritize traditional roles over formal education, particularly for girls. This can result in lower educational attainment for certain demographics.

+ **Quality of Instruction:** Even when access to schools is available, the quality of education can vary significantly. A shortage of qualified teachers, inadequate training, and poor infrastructure can compromise the learning experience.

Examples of Initiatives

In response to these challenges, various initiatives have emerged on Planet Nebula aimed at improving access to quality education:

1. **Mobile Education Units:**   To address geographical barriers, the Nebulian government has introduced mobile education units that travel to remote areas, providing educational resources and instruction directly to students. These units are equipped with technology and trained educators to deliver lessons in a variety of subjects.

2. **Scholarships and Financial Aid:**   Programs offering scholarships and financial assistance have been implemented to support low-income families. For instance, the Nebulian Education Fund provides financial support to students from disadvantaged backgrounds, enabling them to attend quality schools without the burden of excessive costs.

3. **Community Engagement Programs:**   Initiatives that involve community leaders and parents in educational planning have been established to address cultural barriers. By promoting the value of education and encouraging parental involvement, these programs aim to shift perceptions about education and its importance for all children.

4. **Teacher Training and Development:**   To enhance the quality of instruction, the Nebulian government has invested in teacher training programs. These initiatives focus on professional development, equipping educators with modern teaching techniques and resources to improve classroom outcomes.

Conclusion

Access to quality education on Planet Nebula remains a multifaceted challenge that requires a comprehensive approach. By understanding the theoretical frameworks of Human Capital and Social Justice, recognizing the barriers faced by various communities, and implementing targeted initiatives, Nebula can move towards a more equitable educational landscape. Ensuring that every individual has the opportunity to receive a quality education is not only a moral imperative but also a necessary investment in the future prosperity of Nebulian society.

Vocational training and lifelong learning

Vocational training and lifelong learning have emerged as critical components of the social policy reforms on Planet Nebula, addressing the ever-changing demands of a dynamic economy and the diverse needs of its populace. In this section, we will explore the theoretical underpinnings of vocational training, the challenges faced in its implementation, and the successful examples that have emerged from Nebula's approach to lifelong learning.

Theoretical Framework

Vocational training is grounded in several educational theories, primarily the constructivist approach, which posits that learners construct knowledge through experiences and reflection. According to [?], experiential learning is a process whereby knowledge is created through the transformation of experience. This theory is particularly relevant for vocational training, which emphasizes hands-on experience and skill acquisition in specific trades or professions.

Furthermore, the concept of lifelong learning, as articulated by [?], extends beyond formal education to encompass all learning activities undertaken throughout life, aimed at improving knowledge, skills, and competencies. This perspective aligns with the needs of a rapidly evolving job market where continuous skill enhancement is essential for employability.

Challenges in Implementation

Despite the theoretical benefits, several challenges hinder the effective implementation of vocational training and lifelong learning programs on Planet Nebula:

- **Funding and Resources:** Many vocational training programs struggle with inadequate funding, limiting access to quality training facilities and qualified instructors. The government must allocate sufficient resources to ensure that these programs can thrive.

- **Public Perception:** There is often a stigma attached to vocational training, viewed as a lesser alternative to traditional academic pathways. This perception can deter individuals from pursuing vocational education, leading to a skills gap in the labor market.

- **Alignment with Industry Needs:** Vocational training programs must adapt to the evolving demands of the job market. A disconnect between educational institutions and industry can result in graduates lacking the necessary skills for employment.

- **Access and Equity:** Geographic and socio-economic disparities can limit access to vocational training. Marginalized communities may face barriers such as transportation, affordability, and lack of information about available programs.

Examples of Successful Implementation

To address these challenges, several initiatives on Planet Nebula have demonstrated the potential of vocational training and lifelong learning:

+ **The Nebulian Skills Academy:** This institution has successfully integrated industry partnerships into its curriculum, ensuring that training programs are tailored to current job market needs. By collaborating with local businesses, the academy provides apprenticeships that offer students real-world experience while helping companies fill skill gaps.

+ **Online Learning Platforms:** In response to the need for flexible learning options, Nebula has seen the rise of online vocational training platforms. These platforms provide access to a wide range of courses, allowing learners to acquire new skills at their own pace, regardless of their location. The success of platforms such as NebulaLearn has increased enrollment in vocational programs by 30% over the past three years.

+ **Community-Based Initiatives:** Various grassroots organizations have launched community-driven vocational training programs aimed at marginalized populations. These initiatives not only provide training but also foster a sense of community and support among participants, enhancing their chances of successful employment.

+ **Government Incentives:** The Nebulian government has implemented tax incentives for businesses that invest in employee training programs. This policy encourages companies to prioritize the continuous development of their workforce, leading to a more skilled and adaptable labor force.

Conclusion

In conclusion, vocational training and lifelong learning are vital components of Nebula's social policy reforms, addressing the skills gap and promoting economic growth. While challenges remain, successful examples demonstrate that with adequate funding, public awareness, and alignment with industry needs, vocational training can empower individuals and strengthen the Nebulian economy. As the society continues to evolve, embracing these educational approaches will be essential for fostering a skilled workforce capable of navigating the complexities of the future.

Healthcare System Overhaul

Universal healthcare implementation

Universal healthcare (UHC) is a system that aims to provide all individuals with access to necessary health services without the risk of financial hardship. The implementation of UHC on Planet Nebula has been a complex process influenced by various socio-political and economic factors. This section explores the theoretical foundations, challenges, and examples of UHC implementation on Nebula.

Theoretical Foundations

The concept of universal healthcare is grounded in several key theories:

+ **Health as a Human Right:** The World Health Organization (WHO) asserts that health is a fundamental human right. This perspective underlines the moral obligation of governments to ensure access to healthcare for all citizens.

+ **Social Justice Theory:** This theory posits that equitable access to healthcare is essential for achieving social justice. It emphasizes the need to address disparities in health outcomes related to socioeconomic status, ethnicity, and geography.

+ **Economic Efficiency:** Proponents of UHC argue that a healthier population leads to increased productivity and economic growth. According to the Grossman model of health capital, individuals invest in their health to enhance their productivity, thereby contributing to economic development.

Challenges in Implementation

While the theoretical foundations of UHC are compelling, the practical implementation on Planet Nebula has faced several challenges:

+ **Funding and Resource Allocation:** One of the primary challenges is securing adequate funding for UHC. The cost of providing comprehensive healthcare services can be substantial. For instance, the Nebulian government initially allocated only 5% of its GDP to healthcare, which proved insufficient to cover the rising demand for services.

+ **Infrastructure Limitations:** Many regions on Nebula, particularly rural areas, lack the necessary healthcare infrastructure. The absence of hospitals, clinics, and trained healthcare professionals poses significant barriers to accessing care. For example, the rural district of Xylon reported a doctor-to-patient ratio of 1:1,500, far below the recommended standard.

+ **Public Resistance and Misinformation:** The implementation of UHC has also been met with public skepticism. Misinformation regarding the implications of UHC, such as fears of government overreach or reduced quality of care, has fueled resistance. In a recent survey, 40% of Nebulians expressed concerns about long wait times and potential rationing of services.

+ **Political Divisions:** The political landscape on Nebula is fragmented, with varying opinions on the role of government in healthcare. The Conservative Movement advocates for a market-driven approach, while the Progressive Coalition supports UHC. This division has led to legislative gridlock and delays in policy implementation.

Successful Examples of Implementation

Despite the challenges, several regions on Nebula have successfully implemented UHC initiatives, providing valuable lessons for broader application:

+ **The City of Lumina:** Lumina has established a successful UHC model that combines public funding with private partnerships. The city government funds basic healthcare services through taxation, while private entities manage hospitals and clinics. This hybrid approach has resulted in a 30% reduction in emergency room visits and improved patient satisfaction rates.

+ **The Health Cooperative of Nebula (HCN):** HCN is a community-based organization that provides comprehensive healthcare to its members. By operating on a subscription model, HCN has achieved a high level of member engagement, with 85% of residents participating. The cooperative model has facilitated preventive care and reduced overall healthcare costs by 20%.

+ **Telehealth Initiatives:** In response to infrastructure challenges, several regions have adopted telehealth services, enabling patients to access care remotely. The Nebulian Ministry of Health reported that telehealth consultations increased by 150% during the implementation phase, significantly improving access for rural populations.

Conclusion

The implementation of universal healthcare on Planet Nebula represents a significant shift in governance and public policy. While the theoretical underpinnings of UHC advocate for equitable access to health services, the practical challenges of funding, infrastructure, public perception, and political divisions must be addressed to achieve successful implementation. By learning from successful examples and adapting strategies to local contexts, Nebula can move closer to realizing the goal of universal healthcare for all its citizens.

$$UHC\ Success = f(\text{Funding, Infrastructure, Public Engagement, Political Will}) \tag{37}$$

Where:

+ Funding represents the financial resources allocated to healthcare.

+ Infrastructure denotes the availability of healthcare facilities and professionals.

+ Public Engagement reflects the level of community involvement and acceptance of UHC.

+ Political Will indicates the commitment of political leaders to support UHC initiatives.

Public-private partnerships in healthcare

Public-private partnerships (PPPs) in healthcare represent a collaborative agreement between government entities and private sector organizations to finance, design, implement, and manage healthcare projects. These partnerships have gained traction on Planet Nebula as a means to enhance the efficiency, accessibility, and quality of healthcare services. This section will explore the theoretical foundations of PPPs, the challenges they face, and notable examples from Nebula.

Theoretical Foundations of PPPs

The concept of public-private partnerships is grounded in several theoretical frameworks, including transaction cost economics, principal-agent theory, and public choice theory. Transaction cost economics posits that partnerships can reduce the costs associated with public service delivery by leveraging private sector efficiencies. According to [?], the alignment of incentives between public and private entities can lead to improved service outcomes.

Principal-agent theory, as articulated by [?], highlights the relationship dynamics between public authorities (principals) and private contractors (agents). The challenge lies in ensuring that agents act in the best interests of the principals, which necessitates robust monitoring and accountability mechanisms.

Public choice theory, on the other hand, suggests that government officials may prioritize personal or political gains over the public good. PPPs can mitigate this by introducing competitive pressures and performance-based incentives, thereby aligning the interests of both sectors towards achieving common healthcare goals [?].

Challenges of PPPs in Healthcare

Despite their potential benefits, PPPs in healthcare face several challenges:

1. **Inequitable Access**: One of the primary concerns with PPPs is the risk of exacerbating health inequalities. Private entities may prioritize profit maximization, leading to reduced access for marginalized populations. As noted by [?], this can result in a two-tiered healthcare system where affluent citizens receive superior services while the disadvantaged are left with inadequate care.

2. **Quality Control**: Ensuring consistent quality in healthcare services delivered through PPPs can be problematic. The reliance on private providers may lead to variations in service standards, as profit motives can conflict with the ethical obligations of healthcare delivery [?].

3. **Transparency and Accountability**: The complexity of PPP arrangements can obscure accountability. Issues related to transparency in decision-making processes and financial transactions may arise, leading to public distrust. As highlighted by [?], the lack of clear governance structures can hinder effective oversight.

4. **Long-term Sustainability**: The sustainability of PPPs is often questioned, particularly in terms of long-term financial commitments. Governments may struggle to maintain funding levels once initial contracts expire, potentially jeopardizing the continuity of care [?].

Examples of PPPs in Healthcare on Planet Nebula

Several noteworthy examples of PPPs in healthcare on Planet Nebula illustrate both the potential benefits and pitfalls of such arrangements:
  - **Nebula Health Initiative (NHI)**: Launched in 2021, the NHI is a collaboration between the Nebulian government and a consortium of private healthcare providers. The initiative aims to expand access to primary healthcare services in rural areas. Initial reports indicate a 30% increase in healthcare utilization in these regions. However, concerns have been raised regarding the adequacy of service quality, with some patients reporting dissatisfaction with care received [?].
  - **Nebula Medical Technology Partnership (NMTP)**: This partnership focuses on integrating advanced medical technologies into public healthcare facilities. By leveraging private sector innovation, the NMTP has successfully implemented telemedicine services across several hospitals. While this has improved access to specialist care, issues surrounding data privacy and cybersecurity have emerged, necessitating ongoing discussions about regulatory frameworks [?].
  - **Emergency Response PPP**: In response to the recent pandemic, the Nebulian government entered into a PPP with a private pharmaceutical company to expedite vaccine development and distribution. This partnership resulted in the rapid rollout of vaccines, significantly reducing infection rates. Nevertheless, the process faced criticism regarding transparency in procurement practices and the prioritization of profit over public health [?].

Conclusion

Public-private partnerships in healthcare on Planet Nebula present a complex interplay of opportunities and challenges. While they can enhance service delivery and foster innovation, careful consideration must be given to issues of equity, quality, and accountability. As Nebula continues to navigate its healthcare landscape, the lessons learned from existing PPPs will be crucial in shaping future governance reforms. Ensuring that these partnerships prioritize the public good over profit will be essential for achieving a sustainable and equitable healthcare system.

Addressing healthcare disparities

Healthcare disparities refer to the differences in access to or availability of healthcare services among various population groups. These disparities often correlate with socioeconomic status, geographic location, race, and ethnicity, leading to unequal health outcomes. Addressing these disparities is critical for ensuring equitable health for all citizens on Planet Nebula.

Theoretical Framework

The theoretical framework for understanding healthcare disparities can be grounded in several key theories:

- **Social Determinants of Health (SDH):** This theory posits that health outcomes are influenced not only by medical care but also by social and economic factors. These determinants include education, income, employment, social support, and community safety. The SDH model highlights that individuals with lower socioeconomic status often face barriers to accessing quality healthcare.

- **Health Equity Theory:** This theory emphasizes that everyone should have a fair opportunity to attain their full health potential. Health equity is achieved when disparities in health outcomes are eliminated, and this requires systemic changes in policies and practices that contribute to these disparities.

- **Intersectionality:** This framework recognizes that individuals may experience overlapping social identities (e.g., race, gender, class) that can compound their disadvantages in accessing healthcare. Intersectionality highlights the need for tailored approaches to address the unique challenges faced by different groups.

Problems Contributing to Healthcare Disparities

Several factors contribute to healthcare disparities on Planet Nebula:

1. **Economic Barriers:** Individuals from lower-income backgrounds often lack health insurance or face high out-of-pocket costs, which prevent them from seeking necessary medical care. A study conducted in the Central Nebulian region found that 40% of low-income residents reported delaying medical treatment due to cost concerns.

2. **Geographic Barriers:** Rural populations on Nebula may face significant challenges in accessing healthcare services due to distance from healthcare facilities. For instance, in the Northern Highlands, residents may need to

travel over 100 kilometers to reach the nearest hospital, resulting in delayed or foregone care.

3. **Cultural and Linguistic Barriers:** Minority populations may encounter difficulties in navigating the healthcare system due to language differences or cultural misunderstandings. For example, the Zynari community, which primarily speaks a dialect not commonly used in medical settings, reported feeling alienated and misunderstood during healthcare visits.

4. **Discrimination and Bias:** Implicit biases among healthcare providers can lead to substandard treatment for marginalized groups. Research indicates that Nebulian healthcare providers may unconsciously hold stereotypes that affect their clinical decision-making, resulting in disparities in treatment options offered to different demographic groups.

Examples of Initiatives to Address Disparities

Several initiatives have been implemented on Planet Nebula to address healthcare disparities:

+ **Community Health Programs:** The Nebulian government has established community health programs aimed at increasing access to care in underserved areas. For example, mobile health clinics have been deployed to rural regions, providing essential services such as vaccinations, screenings, and health education.

+ **Telemedicine Expansion:** The rise of telemedicine has provided a new avenue for individuals in remote areas to access healthcare services. The Nebulian Ministry of Health reported a 150% increase in telehealth consultations over the past year, particularly benefiting those who may have difficulty traveling to healthcare facilities.

+ **Cultural Competency Training:** Healthcare providers are undergoing training programs designed to enhance cultural competency and reduce implicit bias. These training sessions focus on understanding the unique needs of diverse populations, which has shown promise in improving patient-provider relationships and health outcomes.

+ **Policy Reforms:** The Nebulian government has introduced policies aimed at expanding health insurance coverage, particularly for low-income families. The implementation of a universal healthcare model has significantly reduced the percentage of uninsured individuals, from 15% to 5% in just two years.

Measuring Progress

To assess the effectiveness of initiatives aimed at reducing healthcare disparities, several metrics can be utilized:

$$\text{Health Equity Index (HEI)} = \frac{\text{Access to Care Score}}{\text{Health Outcome Score}} \qquad (38)$$

The HEI provides a quantitative measure of health equity by comparing access to care against actual health outcomes. A higher HEI indicates improved equity in healthcare access and outcomes.

Additionally, regular surveys and community feedback mechanisms can be established to gauge public perception of healthcare services and identify ongoing barriers to access.

Conclusion

Addressing healthcare disparities on Planet Nebula is an ongoing challenge that requires a multifaceted approach. By understanding the theoretical underpinnings of these disparities and implementing targeted initiatives, the government and healthcare providers can work towards achieving health equity. Continuous evaluation of policies and practices will be essential in ensuring that all Nebulians have access to the care they need, regardless of their socioeconomic status, geographic location, or cultural background.

Social Justice Initiatives

Equal rights and anti-discrimination laws

The concept of equal rights and anti-discrimination laws on Planet Nebula has evolved significantly over the past few decades. As Nebulian society became increasingly diverse, the necessity for legal frameworks that promote equality and protect against discrimination became paramount. This section explores the theoretical foundations, existing problems, and notable examples of equal rights and anti-discrimination laws in Nebula.

Theoretical Foundations

The theoretical underpinning of equal rights is rooted in the principles of justice and fairness. Philosophers like John Rawls have argued for the "veil of ignorance" as a method for determining the justice of societal structures. Under this theory, decision-makers must consider policies as if they do not know their own social status, gender, or ethnicity, promoting a more equitable approach to governance.

The principle of equality before the law, as articulated by legal theorists such as Ronald Dworkin, emphasizes that every individual should be treated equally by legal institutions. This principle is crucial in the formulation of anti-discrimination laws, which aim to eradicate biases based on race, gender, sexual orientation, disability, and other characteristics.

Current Problems

Despite the robust framework of equal rights and anti-discrimination laws, significant challenges persist on Planet Nebula. One of the most pressing issues is the enforcement of these laws. Many Nebulians still face discrimination in various sectors, including employment, housing, and education.

$$\text{Discrimination Rate} = \frac{\text{Number of Discrimination Cases}}{\text{Total Population}} \times 100 \qquad (39)$$

For example, recent studies have shown that approximately 15% of Nebulians reported experiencing some form of discrimination in the workplace, indicating that enforcement mechanisms may be insufficient.

Additionally, the cultural attitudes towards marginalized groups can hinder the effectiveness of anti-discrimination laws. While legislation may exist, societal norms and prejudices can perpetuate discriminatory practices. This is particularly evident in rural areas, where traditional views may prevail over progressive legal frameworks.

Examples of Legislation

Nebula has implemented several key pieces of legislation aimed at promoting equal rights and combating discrimination:

+ **The Equal Rights Act (ERA):** Enacted in 2045, the ERA prohibits discrimination on the basis of gender and sexual orientation. It mandates equal pay for equal work and provides legal recourse for those who experience gender-based discrimination.

+ **The Nebulian Anti-Discrimination Act (NADA):** This comprehensive legislation, passed in 2050, addresses discrimination based on race, ethnicity, religion, and disability. NADA established the Nebulian Equality Commission, which is responsible for investigating complaints and enforcing anti-discrimination laws.

+ **The Disability Inclusion Act (DIA):** Enacted in 2060, this law ensures that individuals with disabilities have equal access to public spaces, education, and employment. It mandates reasonable accommodations in workplaces and educational institutions.

Impact of Legislation

The impact of these laws has been significant, yet uneven. The ERA has led to a notable increase in women's participation in the workforce, with female employment rates rising from 45% in 2040 to 60% in 2060. However, challenges remain in achieving equal pay, as the gender wage gap persists, with women earning approximately 80% of what their male counterparts earn for similar roles.

The NADA has also had a transformative effect, with reported cases of racial discrimination decreasing by 30% since its implementation. Nonetheless, systemic racism continues to be a challenge, particularly among minority communities who often face barriers to accessing justice.

Conclusion and Recommendations

In conclusion, while Planet Nebula has made significant strides in establishing equal rights and anti-discrimination laws, ongoing challenges necessitate continued efforts in enforcement, education, and cultural change.

To enhance the effectiveness of these laws, the following recommendations are proposed:

+ **Strengthening Enforcement Mechanisms:** Increasing funding and resources for the Nebulian Equality Commission to ensure timely investigations and interventions in discrimination cases.

+ **Public Awareness Campaigns:** Implementing educational programs aimed at changing societal attitudes toward marginalized groups, focusing on the benefits of diversity and inclusion.

+ **Data Collection and Transparency:** Establishing comprehensive data collection on discrimination cases to better understand the scope of the problem and evaluate the effectiveness of existing laws.

By addressing these issues, Nebula can move closer to achieving true equality and justice for all its inhabitants.

Gender equality and women's empowerment

Gender equality and women's empowerment are fundamental components of a just and equitable society on Planet Nebula. The pursuit of gender equality involves ensuring that individuals of all genders have equal rights, responsibilities, and opportunities. Women's empowerment refers to the process of increasing the spiritual, political, social, educational, gender, or economic strength of individuals and communities, particularly women. This section explores the theoretical frameworks, challenges, and examples of gender equality initiatives on Planet Nebula.

Theoretical Frameworks

Several theoretical frameworks underpin the discourse on gender equality and women's empowerment:

- **Social Feminism:** This theory posits that women's oppression is rooted in both capitalism and patriarchy. It emphasizes the need for systemic change to achieve gender equality. Social feminists advocate for policies that address both economic and social inequalities, such as equal pay and access to education.

- **Intersectionality:** Coined by Kimberlé Crenshaw, intersectionality highlights how various forms of discrimination (based on race, class, sexuality, etc.) intersect and affect women's experiences. This framework is crucial for understanding the diverse challenges faced by women on Planet Nebula, as it calls for an inclusive approach to policy-making.

- **Capability Approach:** Developed by Amartya Sen and Martha Nussbaum, this approach focuses on enhancing individuals' capabilities and opportunities. It emphasizes that true empowerment involves enabling women to lead lives they value, which includes access to education, healthcare, and economic resources.

Challenges to Gender Equality

Despite significant progress, several challenges hinder the achievement of gender equality on Planet Nebula:

- **Cultural Norms and Stereotypes:** Deeply entrenched cultural norms often dictate gender roles, limiting women's opportunities in education and employment. For instance, in some Nebulian communities, traditional beliefs prioritize male education over female education, perpetuating cycles of poverty and inequality.

+ **Violence Against Women:** Gender-based violence remains a pervasive issue. According to recent studies, approximately 30% of women on Planet Nebula have experienced some form of physical or sexual violence. This violence not only affects women's physical and mental health but also restricts their participation in public life.

+ **Economic Disparities:** Women in Nebula often face economic disadvantages, including wage gaps and limited access to financial resources. The gender pay gap is estimated to be around 20%, with women earning significantly less than their male counterparts for similar work. This economic inequality hampers women's empowerment and independence.

Examples of Gender Equality Initiatives

Several initiatives have been implemented on Planet Nebula to promote gender equality and empower women:

+ **Legislative Reforms:** The Nebulian government has enacted laws aimed at promoting gender equality, such as the Gender Equality Act, which mandates equal pay for equal work and prohibits discrimination based on gender in employment. These legal frameworks are essential for creating a more equitable society.

+ **Education Programs:** Various NGOs and governmental organizations have launched education initiatives targeting young girls. Programs such as "Girls' Rise," which provides scholarships and mentorship for girls in underserved areas, have significantly increased female enrollment in schools. As a result, the enrollment rate of girls in secondary education has risen from 40% to 65% over the past decade.

+ **Women's Economic Empowerment Programs:** Initiatives like "Nebula Women in Business" support female entrepreneurs through training, microloans, and networking opportunities. These programs have helped thousands of women start their businesses, contributing to economic growth and reducing poverty levels in their communities.

Impact of Gender Equality on Society

The promotion of gender equality and women's empowerment has far-reaching implications for Nebulian society:

- **Economic Growth:** Research indicates that closing the gender gap in labor force participation could increase Nebula's GDP by up to 10%. Empowering women economically leads to increased productivity and innovation, benefiting the entire economy.

- **Social Cohesion:** Gender equality fosters social cohesion and stability. Societies that prioritize gender equality tend to experience lower levels of violence and conflict, as empowered women are more likely to engage in community-building activities and advocate for peaceful resolutions.

- **Health Outcomes:** Women's empowerment is linked to improved health outcomes for families and communities. Educated women are more likely to make informed health choices, leading to lower maternal and child mortality rates. For instance, maternal mortality rates on Planet Nebula have decreased by 25% in regions where women's health education programs have been implemented.

Conclusion

In conclusion, gender equality and women's empowerment are critical for achieving a just and equitable society on Planet Nebula. While significant challenges remain, the ongoing efforts to promote gender equality through legislative reforms, education initiatives, and economic empowerment programs are paving the way for a brighter future. By addressing the root causes of gender inequality and fostering an inclusive society, Planet Nebula can harness the full potential of its diverse population, ultimately leading to sustainable development and social harmony.

$$\text{Gender Equality Index} = \frac{\text{Women Empowerment Score}}{\text{Total Population}} \times 100 \qquad (40)$$

Racial and Ethnic Diversity Inclusion

The inclusion of racial and ethnic diversity in governance is not merely a matter of representation; it is a fundamental principle that enriches policy-making and strengthens societal cohesion. On Planet Nebula, the journey towards embracing racial and ethnic diversity has been fraught with challenges, yet it has also provided valuable lessons in the pursuit of a more equitable society.

Theoretical Framework

The importance of diversity can be understood through several theoretical lenses. Social identity theory posits that individuals derive a sense of identity from the groups to which they belong, influencing their perceptions and interactions with others [?]. In governance, this implies that diverse representation can lead to more comprehensive and inclusive policies, as decision-makers bring varied perspectives and experiences to the table.

Furthermore, the contact hypothesis suggests that increased interaction between diverse groups can reduce prejudice and foster understanding [?]. This theory underlines the need for inclusive governance structures that facilitate dialogue and cooperation among different racial and ethnic communities.

Challenges in Racial and Ethnic Inclusion

Despite the theoretical benefits, the practical implementation of racial and ethnic diversity in governance on Planet Nebula has encountered significant obstacles. Historical injustices, systemic discrimination, and socio-economic disparities have created an environment where marginalized groups often find themselves excluded from political processes.

One of the primary challenges is the underrepresentation of minority groups in political institutions. For instance, while the Progressive Coalition promotes diversity, the Centrist Party has been criticized for its lack of minority candidates in key positions. This disparity is reflected in electoral outcomes, where certain demographics are disproportionately represented in government, leading to policies that may not address the needs of all citizens.

Additionally, there exists a pervasive issue of tokenism, where individuals from marginalized communities are included in decision-making processes without genuine power or influence. This often results in a superficial approach to diversity, undermining the potential for meaningful change.

Examples of Inclusion Initiatives

In response to these challenges, several initiatives have been launched on Planet Nebula aimed at promoting racial and ethnic diversity in governance. One notable example is the establishment of the *Diversity and Inclusion Council*, which aims to ensure that all racial and ethnic groups are represented in policy discussions. This council has implemented outreach programs to engage underrepresented communities, encouraging them to participate in the political process.

Another initiative is the introduction of *equity audits* in government agencies, which assess the impact of policies on different racial and ethnic groups. These audits aim to identify disparities and recommend changes to ensure that all citizens benefit equally from government programs. For example, a recent audit revealed that healthcare access was disproportionately limited for certain ethnic minorities, prompting reforms to address these inequities.

Case Study: The Community Empowerment Program

The *Community Empowerment Program* (CEP) serves as a case study in effective racial and ethnic inclusion. Launched in response to growing demands for equitable representation, the CEP focuses on empowering marginalized communities through education, advocacy, and direct participation in governance.

The program has successfully trained over 500 community leaders from diverse backgrounds, equipping them with the skills necessary to engage in political advocacy and influence policy decisions. Participants have reported increased confidence in their ability to affect change, leading to a rise in voter turnout among minority populations.

Moreover, the CEP has fostered partnerships with local organizations, creating a network of support that amplifies the voices of underrepresented groups. This collaborative approach has led to significant policy changes, such as the implementation of anti-discrimination laws and increased funding for community health initiatives.

Conclusion and Future Directions

The journey towards racial and ethnic diversity inclusion on Planet Nebula is ongoing, marked by both progress and setbacks. While initiatives like the Diversity and Inclusion Council and the Community Empowerment Program demonstrate the potential for meaningful change, challenges remain. It is essential for governance structures to prioritize diversity not only as a goal but as a core principle that informs all aspects of policy-making.

Looking forward, the integration of diversity metrics into governance frameworks could provide a more systematic approach to evaluating progress. Additionally, fostering intergroup dialogue and collaboration will be crucial in building trust and understanding among diverse communities.

Ultimately, the success of racial and ethnic diversity inclusion on Planet Nebula will depend on the commitment of all stakeholders to create an inclusive society where every voice is heard and valued. As Nebulian society continues to evolve, it is imperative that the lessons learned from past struggles inform future governance reforms, ensuring that diversity is not just an aspiration but a reality.

Technological Advancements and Governance

Technological Advancements and Governance

Technological Advancements and Governance

The intersection of technological advancements and governance has become a pivotal area of study and implementation on Planet Nebula. As societies evolve, so too do the tools and systems that govern them. This section examines the impact of technological advancements on governance structures, highlighting both theoretical frameworks and practical examples that illustrate the complexities involved.

Theoretical Frameworks

Governance, in its essence, refers to the processes and structures through which societies organize themselves, make decisions, and enforce rules. The incorporation of technology into governance can be understood through several theoretical lenses:

- **Network Governance Theory:** This theory posits that governance is increasingly characterized by networks of actors rather than hierarchical structures. Technology facilitates these networks by enabling real-time communication and collaboration across various stakeholders, including government agencies, private sector actors, and civil society.

- **E-Governance Theory:** E-governance emphasizes the use of digital tools to enhance the efficiency, transparency, and accessibility of government services. It encompasses a range of applications, from online voting systems to digital public service delivery, aiming to bridge the gap between citizens and their governments.

+ **Technological Determinism:** This perspective suggests that technological advancements shape social structures and cultural values. In the context of governance, this implies that the adoption of new technologies can fundamentally alter the dynamics of power and authority within a society.

Impact of Technological Advancements

The integration of technology into governance on Planet Nebula has led to several significant impacts:

1. **Increased Efficiency:** Automation and data analytics have streamlined bureaucratic processes, reducing the time and resources required for decision-making. For example, the Nebulian government implemented an AI-driven system that analyzes public feedback on policies, allowing for quicker adjustments based on citizen input.

2. **Enhanced Transparency:** Technologies such as blockchain have been utilized to create transparent systems for public spending and resource allocation. By providing an immutable record of transactions, these technologies help to reduce corruption and increase public trust in government institutions.

3. **Citizen Engagement:** Social media platforms and mobile applications have revolutionized how citizens interact with their governments. Initiatives such as the "Nebula Connect" app allow citizens to report issues, propose policy changes, and engage in discussions with elected officials, fostering a more participatory governance model.

Challenges and Problems

Despite the advantages, the integration of technology into governance also presents several challenges:

+ **Digital Divide:** While technology can enhance governance, it can also exacerbate existing inequalities. Not all citizens have equal access to digital tools, leading to disparities in participation and representation. This digital divide can hinder the effectiveness of e-governance initiatives.

+ **Data Privacy Concerns:** The collection and analysis of vast amounts of data raise significant privacy issues. Citizens may be wary of how their data is used, leading to distrust in governmental institutions. The Nebulian government has faced criticism over its data collection practices, prompting calls for stricter regulations.

+ **Cybersecurity Threats:** As governance systems become more reliant on technology, they also become more vulnerable to cyberattacks. The potential for data breaches and system failures poses risks to national security and public safety. For instance, a recent cyberattack on Nebula's central data repository compromised sensitive information, leading to widespread panic and calls for improved cybersecurity measures.

Examples of Technological Integration in Governance

Several notable examples illustrate the successful integration of technology into governance on Planet Nebula:

+ **Smart City Initiatives:** Cities across Nebula have adopted smart technologies to improve urban governance. For example, the city of Nebulopolis implemented an IoT-based traffic management system that optimizes traffic flow and reduces congestion. This system utilizes real-time data from sensors and cameras to adjust traffic signals dynamically.

+ **AI in Policy Formulation:** The Nebulian government has begun employing AI algorithms to assist in policy formulation. These algorithms analyze large datasets to identify trends and predict outcomes, enabling policymakers to make informed decisions. However, concerns about the lack of transparency in these algorithms have sparked debates about accountability in governance.

+ **Digital Voting Systems:** In response to declining voter turnout, Nebula introduced a digital voting system that allows citizens to cast their votes online. While this innovation increased participation, it also raised concerns about the security and integrity of the electoral process.

Conclusion

The relationship between technological advancements and governance on Planet Nebula is complex and multifaceted. While technology has the potential to enhance efficiency, transparency, and citizen engagement, it also presents significant challenges that must be addressed. As Nebula continues to navigate the evolving landscape of governance, it is imperative that policymakers strike a balance between leveraging technological innovations and safeguarding democratic values.

In summary, the integration of technology into governance is not merely a trend; it is a fundamental shift that will shape the future of Nebulian society. By embracing these advancements while remaining vigilant about their implications, Nebula can pave the way for a more effective and inclusive governance framework.

Artificial Intelligence in Decision-making

AI algorithms in policy formulation

In recent years, the integration of Artificial Intelligence (AI) into the policy formulation process has emerged as a transformative approach for governance on Planet Nebula. AI algorithms, leveraging vast datasets and sophisticated computational techniques, have the potential to enhance decision-making, improve efficiency, and provide insights that were previously unattainable. This section delves into the theoretical underpinnings of AI in policy formulation, the challenges it presents, and practical examples from Nebula's governance landscape.

Theoretical Framework

AI algorithms in policy formulation are grounded in several theoretical frameworks, including data-driven decision-making, predictive analytics, and machine learning. These frameworks enable policymakers to analyze complex datasets and derive actionable insights. At the core of this approach is the concept of *predictive modeling*, which utilizes historical data to forecast future outcomes. The general form of a predictive model can be expressed mathematically as:

$$Y = f(X) + \epsilon \tag{41}$$

where Y represents the outcome variable (e.g., public health indicators), X denotes a vector of predictor variables (e.g., demographic data, economic factors), f is the function that describes the relationship between Y and X, and ϵ is the error term capturing the variability not explained by the model.

Machine learning techniques, such as decision trees and neural networks, are particularly relevant in this context. These algorithms can identify patterns in data that traditional statistical methods may overlook, thereby enhancing the accuracy of policy predictions. For instance, a neural network can be employed to model the impact of various social policies on income inequality, allowing policymakers to simulate potential outcomes before implementing changes.

Challenges in Implementation

Despite the promising potential of AI algorithms in policy formulation, several challenges hinder their effective implementation.

Data Quality and Availability   The efficacy of AI algorithms is heavily reliant on the quality and comprehensiveness of the data used. In many instances, datasets may be incomplete, biased, or outdated. For example, if a dataset lacks representation from marginalized communities, any policy recommendations derived from such data may perpetuate existing inequalities.

Algorithmic Bias   Another significant concern is the risk of algorithmic bias, where AI systems inadvertently reinforce societal biases present in the training data. This phenomenon can lead to discriminatory outcomes in policy formulation, particularly in areas such as criminal justice or healthcare. A notable case on Planet Nebula involved an AI system used to allocate healthcare resources, which disproportionately favored affluent regions due to historical healthcare access disparities.

Transparency and Accountability   The opacity of AI algorithms poses a challenge for transparency in governance.   Policymakers and the public may struggle to understand how decisions are made, leading to skepticism and distrust. Establishing clear accountability mechanisms is essential to ensure that AI-driven policies can be scrutinized and held to ethical standards.

Practical Examples

Several initiatives on Planet Nebula have successfully integrated AI algorithms into policy formulation, showcasing both the potential benefits and the challenges faced.

Public Health Policy   During the recent health crisis, the Nebulian government employed AI algorithms to analyze the spread of infectious diseases. By utilizing real-time data from various sources, including hospitals and social media, the algorithms were able to predict outbreak hotspots with remarkable accuracy. This predictive capability enabled the government to allocate resources effectively and implement targeted interventions, ultimately saving lives.

Urban Planning   In urban planning, AI algorithms have been utilized to optimize traffic flow and reduce congestion in major cities. By analyzing traffic patterns and environmental data, AI systems can recommend infrastructure improvements and policy changes that enhance urban mobility. For instance, an AI-driven analysis in the city of Nebulopolis led to the implementation of smart traffic signals that adapt to real-time traffic conditions, significantly reducing commute times.

Environmental Policy   AI algorithms have also played a crucial role in formulating environmental policies aimed at combating climate change.   By processing vast amounts of environmental data, these algorithms can model the potential impacts of various policy scenarios, such as carbon pricing or renewable energy incentives.   A landmark study on Planet Nebula demonstrated that AI-driven simulations could identify the most effective strategies for reducing carbon emissions while balancing economic growth.

Conclusion

The integration of AI algorithms into policy formulation on Planet Nebula represents a significant advancement in governance. While the potential benefits are substantial, addressing the challenges of data quality, algorithmic bias, and transparency is crucial for ensuring that AI-driven policies are equitable and effective. As Nebula continues to navigate the complexities of modern governance, the lessons learned from AI implementation will inform future approaches to policymaking, ultimately shaping a more responsive and inclusive society.

Ethical concerns and transparency

The integration of artificial intelligence (AI) into decision-making processes on Planet Nebula raises significant ethical concerns and necessitates a commitment to transparency. As AI systems become increasingly capable of influencing policies that affect the lives of Nebulians, understanding the implications of their use is paramount. This section explores the ethical challenges posed by AI in governance, the importance of transparency, and the measures that can be implemented to address these concerns.

Ethical Challenges

One of the primary ethical concerns regarding AI in governance is the potential for bias in algorithmic decision-making. AI systems are trained on historical data, which may reflect existing societal biases. For example, if an AI model used for resource allocation is trained on data that disproportionately favors certain demographics, it may perpetuate inequality rather than alleviate it. The implications of biased algorithms can be profound, leading to decisions that exacerbate social disparities and undermine public trust in governmental institutions.

Moreover, the opacity of AI algorithms poses another ethical dilemma. Many AI models, particularly those based on deep learning, function as "black boxes," making it difficult for stakeholders to understand how decisions are made. This lack of interpretability can lead to a situation where citizens are subjected to decisions without a clear understanding of the rationale behind them, raising concerns about accountability. When individuals cannot comprehend the processes that govern their lives, it erodes their agency and can lead to widespread disenchantment with the political system.

The Importance of Transparency

Transparency in AI governance is crucial for fostering trust between the government and its citizens. By making the workings of AI systems accessible and understandable, governments can demystify the decision-making process and empower citizens to engage with it. Transparency allows for public scrutiny, which can help identify and rectify biases in AI systems. For instance, if a decision made by an AI system is contested, a transparent framework enables stakeholders to investigate the underlying data and algorithms, ensuring accountability.

Furthermore, establishing clear guidelines for the ethical use of AI can help mitigate potential risks. Governments on Planet Nebula can adopt a framework that emphasizes ethical principles such as fairness, accountability, and transparency (FAT). This framework could include the following key components:

- **Bias Mitigation:** Implementing strategies to identify and reduce bias in AI training data and algorithms.

- **Explainability:** Developing models that provide clear explanations for their decisions, enabling users to understand how outcomes are derived.

- **Public Engagement:** Involving citizens in discussions about AI governance, allowing for diverse perspectives to shape policy decisions.

- **Oversight Mechanisms:** Establishing independent bodies to monitor AI systems and ensure compliance with ethical standards.

Examples of Ethical AI Implementation

Several initiatives on Planet Nebula exemplify the successful integration of ethical considerations in AI governance. One notable example is the establishment of the *Nebulian AI Ethics Board*, tasked with reviewing AI applications in public policy. This board comprises ethicists, technologists, and community representatives who assess the potential social impact of AI projects before implementation. By incorporating diverse viewpoints, the board aims to ensure that AI technologies align with the values and needs of Nebulian society.

Another example is the *Open Data Initiative*, which mandates that all data used for AI training be made publicly available. This initiative promotes transparency and allows researchers and citizens to audit the data for biases. By fostering an open environment, the initiative encourages collaboration and innovation while holding the government accountable for its AI applications.

Conclusion

In conclusion, as Planet Nebula continues to embrace AI in governance, addressing ethical concerns and promoting transparency is essential. By recognizing the potential for bias, enhancing the explainability of AI systems, and involving the public in the governance process, Nebulians can harness the benefits of AI while safeguarding democratic values. The path forward requires a commitment to ethical principles and a proactive approach to transparency, ensuring that AI serves as a tool for empowerment rather than oppression.

$$\text{Trust} = \frac{\text{Transparency} + \text{Accountability}}{\text{Bias} + \text{Complexity}} \tag{42}$$

This equation illustrates the relationship between trust, transparency, accountability, bias, and complexity in AI governance. As transparency and accountability increase, trust in AI systems grows, while high levels of bias and complexity diminish trust. Therefore, prioritizing transparency and accountability is crucial for fostering public trust in the governance systems of Planet Nebula.

Public acceptance and accountability

In the ever-evolving landscape of governance on Planet Nebula, the integration of Artificial Intelligence (AI) into decision-making processes has raised critical questions regarding public acceptance and accountability. As AI systems become more prevalent in formulating policies, it is imperative to understand how these technologies are perceived by the populace and the mechanisms that ensure accountability in their deployment.

Public Acceptance of AI in Governance

Public acceptance of AI technologies is influenced by several factors, including trust, perceived benefits, and transparency. According to the Technology Acceptance Model (TAM), which posits that perceived ease of use and perceived usefulness significantly affect users' intentions to adopt technology, these principles are equally applicable to AI in governance contexts.

$$\text{Acceptance} = f(\text{Perceived Usefulness, Perceived Ease of Use}) \qquad (43)$$

For Nebulian citizens, the perceived usefulness of AI in governance may include improved efficiency in public services, enhanced data analysis for policy formulation, and better resource allocation. However, concerns about the complexity of AI systems and the opacity of their algorithms can hinder acceptance. A study conducted by the Nebulian Institute of Technology found that 67% of respondents expressed skepticism towards AI decision-making due to a lack of understanding of how these systems operate.

Challenges to Public Acceptance

Several challenges complicate public acceptance of AI in governance:

+ **Transparency and Explainability:** AI systems often operate as "black boxes," making it difficult for citizens to understand the rationale behind decisions. For example, when AI algorithms were used to allocate healthcare resources during a pandemic, many citizens felt alienated due to the lack of clarity regarding how decisions were made.

+ **Bias and Fairness:** There is a growing concern about inherent biases in AI algorithms, which can perpetuate existing inequalities. In a notable case, an AI system used for social welfare distribution on Planet Nebula was found to favor certain demographic groups, leading to public outcry and demands for accountability.

+ **Job Displacement:** The fear of job loss due to automation can lead to resistance against AI integration. In Nebula, protests erupted when an AI-driven system was introduced to streamline public transportation, resulting in significant layoffs among human operators.

Accountability Mechanisms for AI Governance

To address public concerns and enhance accountability, several mechanisms can be implemented:

- **Regulatory Frameworks:** Establishing clear regulations governing the use of AI in governance is essential. This includes guidelines for transparency, data privacy, and ethical considerations. The Nebulian Council for AI Ethics has proposed a framework that mandates algorithmic transparency and regular audits of AI systems.

- **Public Engagement:** Involving citizens in the decision-making process can foster trust and acceptance. Public forums, workshops, and consultations can help demystify AI technologies and address concerns. The Nebulian government has initiated a series of town hall meetings to discuss AI policies, allowing citizens to voice their opinions and provide feedback.

- **Accountability Mechanisms:** Establishing clear lines of accountability for AI decisions is crucial. This can include creating oversight bodies responsible for monitoring AI applications in governance. The Nebulian AI Oversight Committee, composed of technologists, ethicists, and citizens, has been tasked with ensuring that AI systems operate fairly and transparently.

Case Studies and Examples

Several case studies illustrate the importance of public acceptance and accountability in AI governance:

- **The Healthcare Allocation Algorithm:** In 2022, Nebula implemented an AI system for allocating healthcare resources during a public health crisis. Initially met with skepticism, the system gained acceptance after the government published a detailed report outlining its decision-making process and the data used. This transparency helped alleviate concerns about bias and unfairness.

- **Transportation Automation:** The introduction of AI in public transportation faced significant backlash due to fears of job loss. However, the Nebulian government responded by creating a retraining program for displaced workers, which ultimately led to a more favorable public perception of the AI initiative.

◆ **Citizen Feedback Loops:** The implementation of AI in urban planning included mechanisms for citizen feedback. By allowing residents to provide input on AI-generated proposals, the government enhanced public trust and acceptance of AI-driven decisions.

Conclusion

In conclusion, the successful integration of AI into governance on Planet Nebula hinges on public acceptance and accountability. By addressing concerns related to transparency, bias, and job displacement, and by implementing robust accountability mechanisms, the Nebulian government can foster a more positive relationship between citizens and AI technologies. As governance continues to evolve, the lessons learned from Nebula's experiences with AI can serve as valuable insights for other societies navigating similar challenges in the digital age.

Data Privacy and Cybersecurity

Legal frameworks for data protection

In the age of rapid technological advancement, the importance of robust legal frameworks for data protection cannot be overstated. On Planet Nebula, as in many societies across the universe, the collection, storage, and processing of personal data have raised significant concerns regarding privacy, security, and individual rights. This section delves into the theoretical underpinnings, existing problems, and notable examples of data protection laws on Nebula.

Theoretical Foundations

The theoretical basis for data protection laws is often rooted in the concepts of privacy and autonomy. Privacy, as articulated by theorists such as Westin (1967), is a fundamental human right that allows individuals to control their personal information. This control is essential for maintaining dignity and freedom in a digital age characterized by pervasive surveillance and data collection.

The principle of data minimization, which posits that only the necessary amount of personal data should be collected and processed, is a cornerstone of data protection theory. This principle aligns with the ethical considerations surrounding individual consent and the potential for harm due to misuse of personal data. The legal frameworks on Nebula are designed to reflect these theoretical foundations, aiming to balance the interests of individuals with those of organizations that rely on data for operational purposes.

Existing Problems

Despite the existence of legal frameworks, several challenges persist in the realm of data protection on Planet Nebula. One of the most significant issues is the lack of uniformity in data protection laws across different regions. Nebula is composed of multiple territories, each with its own regulations and enforcement mechanisms. This fragmentation complicates compliance for organizations that operate on a planetary scale, leading to confusion and potential violations.

Moreover, the rapid pace of technological innovation often outstrips the ability of lawmakers to create effective regulations. For instance, the rise of artificial intelligence and machine learning has introduced complexities in data processing that existing laws may not adequately address. The opacity of AI algorithms can hinder individuals' ability to understand how their data is being used, thereby undermining the principle of informed consent.

Another pressing problem is the enforcement of data protection laws. While Nebula has established regulatory bodies tasked with overseeing compliance, these agencies often face resource constraints and lack the authority to impose significant penalties on violators. As a result, organizations may not prioritize data protection, viewing compliance as a mere checkbox rather than a fundamental responsibility.

Notable Examples of Data Protection Laws

On Nebula, the most prominent legal framework for data protection is the Nebulian Data Protection Act (NDPA), enacted in 2020. The NDPA draws inspiration from the General Data Protection Regulation (GDPR) of the Earth, incorporating key principles such as data subject rights, accountability, and transparency. Under the NDPA, individuals have the right to access their personal data, rectify inaccuracies, and request the deletion of their information under certain conditions.

For example, in a landmark case in 2022, a Nebulian citizen successfully sued a major tech company for failing to comply with a data deletion request. The court ruled in favor of the citizen, emphasizing the importance of individual rights in the digital landscape and setting a precedent for future cases.

Another noteworthy initiative is the Nebulian Cybersecurity Framework (NCF), which aims to enhance the security of personal data through risk assessment and management strategies. The NCF mandates that organizations implement robust security measures to protect against data breaches and unauthorized access. However, despite these initiatives, the effectiveness of the NCF is often hampered by inadequate funding and a lack of technical expertise among smaller organizations.

Conclusion

In conclusion, the legal frameworks for data protection on Planet Nebula are crucial in safeguarding individual rights in an increasingly data-driven world. While the NDPA and NCF represent significant strides toward comprehensive data protection, ongoing challenges such as regulatory fragmentation, technological advancements, and enforcement issues must be addressed. Moving forward, it is imperative for Nebulian lawmakers to adapt existing frameworks to keep pace with technological changes and to foster a culture of accountability among organizations handling personal data. Only then can the citizens of Nebula truly enjoy their rights to privacy and data protection in the digital age.

Emerging cybersecurity threats

As Planet Nebula continues to embrace technological advancements, the landscape of cybersecurity threats evolves at an alarming pace. The increasing interconnectivity of systems and the reliance on digital infrastructure expose vulnerabilities that malicious actors exploit. This section delves into the emerging cybersecurity threats that have arisen in the context of Nebula's governance and technological integration.

Theoretical Framework

Cybersecurity threats can be classified into several categories based on their nature and intent. The primary theoretical frameworks used to analyze these threats include the **CIA Triad** (Confidentiality, Integrity, Availability) and the **Kill Chain** model. The CIA Triad emphasizes the need to protect sensitive information from unauthorized access, ensure data integrity, and maintain system availability. The Kill Chain model, developed by Lockheed Martin, outlines the stages of a cyber attack, from reconnaissance to execution, enabling defenders to identify and disrupt attacks at various points.

Types of Emerging Threats

1. **Ransomware Attacks** Ransomware attacks have surged in frequency and sophistication, targeting critical infrastructure and public services. In 2022, a

notorious ransomware group known as *NebulaLock* infiltrated the central data systems of Nebula's healthcare sector, encrypting patient records and demanding a ransom in the form of Nebulian Credits. The aftermath revealed significant vulnerabilities in the cybersecurity protocols of healthcare institutions, leading to calls for stricter regulations and enhanced security measures.

2. Phishing and Social Engineering Phishing attacks, often coupled with social engineering tactics, pose a significant threat to individuals and organizations alike. Attackers exploit human psychology to manipulate targets into revealing sensitive information. A notable incident occurred when employees of the Ministry of Technology fell victim to a sophisticated phishing scheme that masqueraded as an internal communication. The breach compromised sensitive government data and highlighted the need for comprehensive employee training on cybersecurity awareness.

3. Internet of Things (IoT) Vulnerabilities The proliferation of IoT devices has introduced new vulnerabilities that attackers can exploit. Many IoT devices lack robust security features, making them easy targets for cybercriminals. For instance, a security audit revealed that smart meters used for energy management in Nebula's urban areas were susceptible to remote hacking. Attackers could manipulate energy consumption data, leading to financial losses for both consumers and energy providers.

4.   Supply Chain Attacks Supply chain attacks have become increasingly prevalent, as attackers target third-party vendors to gain access to larger organizations. A prominent case involved a breach of the software supply chain used by Nebula's governmental agencies, where malicious code was inserted into a widely-used software update. This incident underscored the necessity for rigorous vetting processes for third-party software and services to mitigate risks.

Problems and Challenges

The emergence of these cybersecurity threats presents several challenges for Nebula's governance:

+ **Resource Allocation:** Allocating sufficient resources for cybersecurity measures is a persistent challenge, particularly in the face of competing public policy priorities. The government must balance investments in cybersecurity with funding for other essential services.

- **Public Awareness:** The general populace often lacks awareness of cybersecurity risks and best practices. This knowledge gap can lead to increased vulnerability, necessitating public education campaigns to promote cybersecurity hygiene.

- **Legislative Framework:** The rapid evolution of technology outpaces legislative efforts to establish comprehensive cybersecurity regulations. Policymakers must adapt existing laws and create new frameworks to address emerging threats effectively.

Examples of Cybersecurity Breaches

To illustrate the severity of these emerging threats, several high-profile cybersecurity breaches on Planet Nebula serve as cautionary tales:

1. **Nebulian Power Grid Attack:** In 2023, a coordinated cyber attack targeted the power grid of Nebula's capital city, resulting in widespread blackouts. The attackers exploited vulnerabilities in the grid's control systems, leading to a significant disruption of public services and raising concerns about national security.

2. **Education Sector Breach:** A breach in the educational database of Nebula's largest university exposed the personal information of thousands of students and faculty members. The incident prompted an investigation into the university's cybersecurity practices and led to a reevaluation of data protection measures across educational institutions.

3. **Government Data Leak:** In a shocking breach, sensitive government documents were leaked online, revealing classified information about Nebula's national security strategies. The incident raised alarms about insider threats and the need for enhanced access controls and monitoring systems.

Conclusion

The landscape of cybersecurity threats on Planet Nebula is complex and continuously evolving. As the society becomes more reliant on technology, it must adopt a proactive approach to cybersecurity that encompasses robust defense mechanisms, public awareness initiatives, and legislative reforms. By addressing the challenges posed by emerging threats, Nebula can safeguard its digital infrastructure and protect its citizens from the detrimental effects of cybercrime.

$$\text{Risk} = \text{Threat} \times \text{Vulnerability} \times \text{Impact} \qquad (44)$$

In conclusion, the equation above encapsulates the essence of cybersecurity risk management. By understanding and mitigating threats, enhancing system vulnerabilities, and minimizing potential impacts, Nebula can fortify its defenses against the ever-present tide of cybersecurity threats.

Balancing privacy rights and national security

The interplay between privacy rights and national security has become a focal point of debate in contemporary governance, particularly on Planet Nebula, where technological advancements have accelerated the collection and analysis of personal data. This section explores the theoretical frameworks, challenges, and practical examples that illustrate the complexities of achieving a balance between safeguarding individual privacy and ensuring national security.

Theoretical Frameworks

At the heart of this debate lies the tension between two fundamental principles: the right to privacy and the imperative of national security. The right to privacy is enshrined in various legal documents and ethical theories, most notably in the *Universal Declaration of Human Rights*, which states that "no one shall be subjected to arbitrary interference with his privacy, family, home or correspondence." Conversely, national security is often justified under the doctrine of *utilitarianism*, where actions are deemed acceptable if they promote the greatest good for the greatest number, even if they infringe on individual rights.

This dichotomy can be mathematically represented by the equation:

$$U = f(P, S)$$

where U is the overall utility derived from a policy, P represents privacy rights, and S signifies national security measures. The goal is to maximize U while minimizing the trade-offs between P and S.

Challenges in Balancing Privacy and Security

1. **Data Surveillance:** The rise of surveillance technologies, such as facial recognition and data mining, poses significant challenges to privacy rights. For instance, the implementation of a planetary-wide surveillance system on Nebula aimed at monitoring potential terrorist activities has raised concerns about mass

surveillance and the erosion of civil liberties. Critics argue that such measures often disproportionately affect marginalized communities, leading to a chilling effect on free expression.

2. **Legal Frameworks:** The legal frameworks governing data protection and national security are often outdated and lack coherence. On Nebula, the *Nebulian Data Protection Act* was enacted to safeguard citizens' privacy; however, it contains numerous exemptions for national security purposes. This has led to ambiguous interpretations and misuse of data by state actors, undermining public trust.

3. **Public Sentiment:** The public's perception of privacy and security is continually evolving. A survey conducted on Nebula revealed that while a majority of citizens support robust national security measures, there is also a strong desire for transparency and accountability in government surveillance practices. The challenge lies in reconciling these often conflicting viewpoints.

Practical Examples

1. **The Nebulian Data Breach Incident:** In 2022, a significant data breach occurred within the Nebulian National Security Agency (NNSA), exposing sensitive personal information of millions of citizens. This incident sparked a nationwide debate about the extent of surveillance and the need for stringent data protection measures. In response, the government initiated a review of its surveillance policies, emphasizing the importance of transparency and citizen oversight.

2. **The Cybersecurity Act of 2023:** In an effort to address the growing concerns regarding data privacy, the Nebulian government passed the Cybersecurity Act of 2023. This legislation aimed to establish clear guidelines for data collection and usage, requiring government agencies to conduct regular audits and report findings to an independent oversight body. While the act was a step towards better privacy protection, critics argue that it still allows for excessive data collection under the guise of national security.

3. **Public Engagement Initiatives:** To foster a more informed public dialogue, various grassroots organizations on Nebula have initiated campaigns advocating for privacy rights. These initiatives include community workshops, public forums, and the use of social media to raise awareness about the implications of government surveillance. By empowering citizens to engage in the policymaking process, these movements strive to create a more balanced approach to privacy and security.

Conclusion

The challenge of balancing privacy rights and national security on Planet Nebula is multifaceted and requires a nuanced approach. As technological advancements continue to shape the landscape of governance, it is imperative for policymakers to adopt frameworks that prioritize both individual rights and collective security. By fostering transparency, accountability, and public engagement, Nebula can strive towards a governance model that respects the dignity of its citizens while safeguarding national interests.

In conclusion, the equation $U = f(P, S)$ serves as a reminder that the quest for optimal governance is an ongoing process, one that necessitates constant evaluation and adaptation to the ever-changing dynamics of society. As Nebula navigates this complex terrain, the lessons learned from its experiences can serve as valuable insights for other societies grappling with similar issues.

Smart Cities and Infrastructure

Sustainable urban development

Sustainable urban development refers to the planning and design of urban spaces that meet the needs of the present without compromising the ability of future generations to meet their own needs. This concept encompasses a wide range of practices and policies aimed at creating resilient, efficient, and equitable cities. The principles of sustainable urban development are rooted in three main pillars: environmental sustainability, economic viability, and social equity.

Theoretical Framework

The theoretical foundation of sustainable urban development is built upon several key theories, including:

- ◆ **Ecological Modernization Theory:** This theory posits that economic growth and environmental protection can be reconciled through technological innovation and policy reform. It suggests that urban areas can become more sustainable by adopting green technologies and practices.

- ◆ **Smart Growth:** This approach advocates for compact, transit-oriented development that reduces urban sprawl and promotes walkability. Smart growth emphasizes mixed-use development, preserving open space, and investing in public transportation systems.

+ **New Urbanism:** This design movement promotes the creation of walkable neighborhoods with a strong sense of community. It emphasizes human-scale development, mixed-use buildings, and public spaces that encourage social interaction.

Problems in Urban Development

Despite the theoretical frameworks supporting sustainable urban development, numerous challenges persist:

+ **Urban Sprawl:** Rapid urbanization often leads to sprawl, characterized by low-density development that consumes vast amounts of land and resources. This phenomenon increases reliance on automobiles, contributing to traffic congestion, air pollution, and greenhouse gas emissions.

+ **Infrastructure Deficits:** Many cities struggle with aging infrastructure that is ill-equipped to handle the demands of a growing population. Inadequate public transportation, water supply, and waste management systems can hinder sustainable development efforts.

+ **Social Inequality:** Sustainable urban development must address social disparities, as marginalized communities often bear the brunt of environmental degradation and lack access to essential services. Ensuring equitable access to housing, transportation, and public spaces is critical for fostering inclusive urban environments.

Examples of Sustainable Urban Development

Several cities around the world have implemented successful sustainable urban development initiatives:

+ **Copenhagen, Denmark:** Known for its ambitious climate goals, Copenhagen aims to become carbon neutral by 2025. The city has invested heavily in cycling infrastructure, public transportation, and green spaces, promoting a high quality of life while reducing emissions.

+ **Portland, Oregon, USA:** Portland is a pioneer in sustainable urban planning, with a focus on compact development and public transit. The city's Urban Growth Boundary restricts sprawl, while its extensive light rail system encourages residents to use public transportation.

+ **Curitiba, Brazil:** Curitiba's innovative Bus Rapid Transit (BRT) system has transformed public transportation in the city, providing efficient and affordable access to residents. The city has also prioritized green spaces, with parks and recreational areas integrated into urban planning.

Conclusion

Sustainable urban development is essential for addressing the pressing challenges of urbanization in the 21st century. By integrating ecological, economic, and social considerations into urban planning, cities can create environments that are not only livable but also resilient to future challenges. As urban areas continue to grow, the adoption of sustainable practices will be crucial for ensuring that they remain vibrant and equitable spaces for all inhabitants.

$$\text{Sustainable Urban Development Index (SUDI)} = \frac{\text{Environmental Performance} + \text{Eco}}{3}$$
(45)

Internet of Things and Automated Systems

The Internet of Things (IoT) refers to the interconnection of everyday objects and devices to the internet, allowing them to send and receive data. On Planet Nebula, the integration of IoT technologies into governance has transformed urban management, resource allocation, and public services. This section explores the theoretical foundations, challenges, and practical applications of IoT and automated systems in Nebulian governance.

Theoretical Foundations

The theoretical underpinnings of IoT can be traced to several key concepts:

+ **Cyber-Physical Systems (CPS):** These systems integrate computation, networking, and physical processes. In Nebula, CPS facilitate real-time monitoring and control of urban infrastructures, such as transportation and energy systems.

+ **Smart Cities Framework:** The smart city concept encompasses the use of IoT to enhance urban living. Nebula's cities have adopted this framework to improve public safety, environmental sustainability, and citizen engagement.

- **Data-Driven Governance:** IoT generates vast amounts of data, which can be analyzed to inform policy decisions. This shift towards data-driven governance allows Nebulian leaders to make more informed choices, though it raises questions about data privacy and ethics.

Challenges of IoT Implementation

While the benefits of IoT are substantial, several challenges hinder its effective implementation in Nebula:

- **Data Privacy and Security:** With the proliferation of connected devices, concerns about data breaches and unauthorized access have escalated. Nebulian citizens are wary of how their data is collected, stored, and utilized. The government must establish robust data protection regulations to address these concerns.

- **Interoperability Issues:** The diversity of IoT devices and platforms can lead to compatibility problems. For instance, if a smart traffic management system cannot communicate with emergency response systems, it could jeopardize public safety. Establishing standardized protocols is crucial for seamless integration.

- **Infrastructure Limitations:** The deployment of IoT technologies requires significant investment in infrastructure. In some regions of Nebula, especially rural areas, the lack of reliable internet connectivity poses a barrier to implementing smart solutions. Addressing these disparities is essential for equitable access to IoT benefits.

Examples of IoT in Nebula

Several initiatives on Planet Nebula exemplify the effective use of IoT and automated systems:

- **Smart Waste Management:** In Nebulian cities, IoT-enabled waste bins equipped with sensors monitor fill levels and optimize collection routes. This system has reduced operational costs by 30% and improved recycling rates by 25%.

- **Automated Traffic Control:** The implementation of smart traffic lights that adapt to real-time traffic conditions has significantly reduced congestion. An analysis showed a 40% decrease in average commute times, leading to lower emissions and improved air quality.

+ **Smart Energy Grids:** Nebula has adopted IoT solutions to create smart energy grids that monitor and manage electricity consumption. These grids enable real-time adjustments based on demand, reducing energy waste by up to 20% and enhancing the integration of renewable energy sources.

Mathematical Modeling of IoT Systems

To quantify the impact of IoT systems, we can use mathematical models. For instance, let C represent the cost savings from implementing an IoT solution, R the reduction in resource consumption, and T the time saved in operational processes. A simplified model can be expressed as:

$$C = aR + bT \tag{46}$$

where a and b are coefficients representing the monetary value of resource savings and time saved, respectively. By analyzing historical data, Nebulian policymakers can calibrate these coefficients to better predict the economic impact of future IoT investments.

Conclusion

The Internet of Things and automated systems present significant opportunities for enhancing governance on Planet Nebula. However, the challenges of data privacy, interoperability, and infrastructure must be addressed to fully realize these benefits. As Nebula continues to evolve technologically, the lessons learned from IoT implementations will be vital for shaping future governance strategies and ensuring that all citizens can partake in the advantages of a connected society.

Citizen engagement and urban governance

Citizen engagement has emerged as a critical component of effective urban governance on Planet Nebula. As cities evolve into complex ecosystems, the need for inclusive decision-making processes becomes paramount. This section explores the theoretical underpinnings of citizen engagement, the challenges faced in its implementation, and successful examples from various Nebulian cities.

Theoretical Framework

The concept of citizen engagement is grounded in several theories of democratic governance and participatory democracy. According to Arnstein's Ladder of Citizen Participation, engagement ranges from manipulation and therapy at the lowest levels to partnership and citizen control at the highest levels [1]. This framework emphasizes the importance of not just informing citizens but actively involving them in the decision-making processes that affect their lives.

Moreover, the Deliberative Democracy theory posits that public discourse and dialogue are essential for informed decision-making [2]. In the context of urban governance, this means creating spaces where citizens can voice their opinions, deliberate on policy options, and contribute to the formulation of urban strategies.

Challenges of Citizen Engagement

Despite the theoretical support for citizen engagement, several challenges hinder its effective implementation in Nebulian cities:

+ **Digital Divide:** Access to technology is uneven across different demographics, leading to disparities in participation. Those without access to the Internet or digital literacy skills may be excluded from online engagement platforms.

+ **Mistrust in Government:** Historical grievances and perceived inefficiencies can lead to skepticism regarding the government's commitment to genuine engagement. Citizens may feel that their contributions are ignored or undervalued.

+ **Complexity of Urban Issues:** Urban governance involves multifaceted issues that can be overwhelming for citizens. Without adequate information and support, meaningful participation becomes challenging.

+ **Tokenism:** Often, engagement initiatives are superficial, merely serving as a means to fulfill legal or political obligations without resulting in real influence over decisions [3].

Successful Examples of Citizen Engagement

Several Nebulian cities have successfully implemented citizen engagement strategies that serve as models for others:

+ **Nebula City's Participatory Budgeting:** In Nebula City, residents are given a direct voice in allocating a portion of the city budget. This initiative has increased transparency and trust in local governance, as citizens can see the direct impact of their decisions on community projects [4].

+ **Greenville's Urban Planning Forums:** Greenville has established regular forums where citizens can discuss urban planning proposals. These forums utilize deliberative techniques to ensure that all voices are heard, fostering a sense of ownership among residents [5].

+ **Data-Driven Decision Making in Starport:** Starport has integrated citizen feedback into its urban governance through data analytics platforms. Citizens can report issues via an app, and the data collected is used to prioritize city services and infrastructure improvements [6].

Conclusion

Citizen engagement is essential for effective urban governance on Planet Nebula. While challenges such as the digital divide, mistrust, and tokenism persist, successful initiatives in cities like Nebula City, Greenville, and Starport demonstrate the potential for meaningful citizen involvement. As urban areas continue to grow and evolve, fostering an engaged citizenry will be crucial for creating responsive and resilient governance structures.

Bibliography

[1] Arnstein, S. R. (1969). A Ladder of Citizen Participation. *Journal of the American Institute of Planners*, 35(4), 216-224.

[2] Habermas, J. (1991). *The Structural Transformation of the Public Sphere: An Inquiry into a Category of Bourgeois Society*. MIT Press.

[3] Cooper, A. (2013). Tokenism in Citizen Engagement: The Case of Urban Governance. *Public Administration Review*, 73(4), 568-577.

[4] Nebula City. (2021). Participatory Budgeting Initiative. Retrieved from [URL].

[5] Greenville Urban Planning Department. (2020). Community Engagement Forums Report. Retrieved from [URL].

[6] Starport Data Analytics Office. (2022). Citizen Feedback Integration in Urban Governance. Retrieved from [URL].

Crisis Management and Emergency Response

Crisis Management and Emergency Response

Crisis Management and Emergency Response

Crisis management and emergency response are critical components of governance on Planet Nebula, where the unique environmental and social dynamics present a variety of challenges. This section will explore the theoretical frameworks, practical problems, and real-world examples that shape the Nebulian approach to crisis management.

Theoretical Frameworks

Crisis management is defined as the process by which an organization prepares for, responds to, and recovers from an unexpected event that threatens to harm the organization or its stakeholders. The theoretical foundations of crisis management can be categorized into several key models:

- **The Four Phases Model:** This model, which includes mitigation, preparedness, response, and recovery, emphasizes a comprehensive approach to managing crises. Each phase plays a crucial role in ensuring that Nebulian society can effectively handle emergencies.

- **The Systems Theory:** This approach views crisis management as a system of interrelated components, including government agencies, NGOs, and the private sector. It highlights the need for coordination and communication among various stakeholders to achieve effective crisis management.

◆ **The Stakeholder Theory:** This theory posits that organizations must consider the interests and needs of all stakeholders during a crisis. On Planet Nebula, this includes citizens, local businesses, and international partners, all of whom play a role in the crisis management process.

Challenges in Crisis Management

Despite the theoretical frameworks in place, Nebulian governance faces several challenges in crisis management:

◆ **Resource Allocation:** Limited resources can hinder effective crisis response. For instance, during the recent seismic activity that affected the western regions of Nebula, local governments struggled to allocate sufficient resources for emergency services, leading to delayed responses and increased casualties.

◆ **Communication Barriers:** Effective communication is essential during a crisis. However, misinformation and communication breakdowns can exacerbate situations. The Nebulian government experienced significant challenges in disseminating accurate information during the pandemic, leading to public confusion and distrust.

◆ **Interagency Coordination:** The complexity of crises often requires collaboration among multiple agencies. The lack of a unified command structure can lead to duplicated efforts or conflicting strategies, as seen during the recent flooding in the central provinces, where various agencies operated independently without a cohesive plan.

Examples of Crisis Management on Planet Nebula

Several notable examples illustrate the successes and failures of crisis management on Planet Nebula:

Natural Disasters: The Nebulian government has implemented early warning systems for natural disasters, particularly for seismic events and tsunamis. These systems utilize advanced technology, including satellite imaging and seismic monitoring, to predict and communicate threats. For example, the early warning system successfully alerted coastal communities of an impending tsunami, allowing for timely evacuations and minimizing loss of life.

Pandemic Response: The COVID-19 pandemic presented unprecedented challenges for Nebulian governance. The government adopted a multi-faceted approach, including widespread testing, contact tracing, and public health campaigns. The implementation of the *Test, Track, and Trace* (T3) strategy was pivotal in controlling the virus's spread. However, initial delays in testing capacity and mixed messaging from authorities led to public skepticism and resistance to health measures.

Terrorism and National Security: In response to rising threats from extremist groups, the Nebulian government has enhanced its counterterrorism measures. This includes intelligence sharing with international partners and community engagement initiatives to prevent radicalization. The establishment of a national security task force has improved coordination among law enforcement agencies, leading to successful interventions in several planned attacks.

Mathematical Models in Crisis Management

Mathematical modeling plays a significant role in crisis management, particularly in forecasting and resource allocation. For example, the use of the following equation can help determine the optimal allocation of resources R:

$$R = \frac{D \times C}{T} \tag{47}$$

where:

+ D is the demand for resources based on the severity of the crisis,

+ C is the capacity of available resources,

+ T is the time available for response.

This equation assists policymakers in making informed decisions about resource distribution during emergencies.

Conclusion

In conclusion, crisis management and emergency response on Planet Nebula are multifaceted processes influenced by various theoretical frameworks, practical challenges, and real-world examples. While the Nebulian government has made significant strides in improving its crisis management capabilities, ongoing challenges such as resource allocation, communication barriers, and interagency coordination require continuous attention and adaptation. By learning from past experiences and leveraging advanced technologies, Nebula can enhance its resilience against future crises, ensuring the safety and well-being of its citizens.

Natural Disaster Preparedness

Early warning systems and evacuation plans

In the context of governance on Planet Nebula, the establishment of effective early warning systems (EWS) and comprehensive evacuation plans is crucial for mitigating the impacts of natural disasters. These systems serve as the first line of defense against catastrophic events, providing timely alerts to populations at risk and facilitating organized evacuations. This section explores the theoretical foundations of EWS, the challenges faced in their implementation, and examples of effective practices observed on Nebula.

Theoretical Foundations of Early Warning Systems

Early warning systems are structured frameworks designed to monitor, analyze, and disseminate information regarding potential hazards. According to the United Nations Office for Disaster Risk Reduction (UNDRR), an effective EWS comprises four key components: (1) **Risk Knowledge**, (2) **Monitoring and Warning Service**, (3) **Dissemination and Communication**, and (4) **Response Capability** [?].

$$EWS = f(RK, MWS, DC, RC) \qquad (48)$$

Where: - EWS = Effectiveness of Early Warning System - RK = Risk Knowledge - MWS = Monitoring and Warning Service - DC = Dissemination and Communication - RC = Response Capability

Risk Knowledge involves identifying hazards, vulnerabilities, and exposure, which is essential for creating accurate risk assessments. This component is foundational, as it informs subsequent stages of the EWS.

Monitoring and Warning Service entails continuous observation of environmental conditions and the issuance of alerts based on predetermined thresholds. For instance, seismic sensors and satellite imagery are employed to detect earthquakes and floods, respectively.

Dissemination and Communication focuses on the methods used to convey warnings to the public. This includes utilizing diverse channels such as social media, traditional media, and community networks to ensure that messages reach all segments of the population.

Response Capability refers to the preparedness of local authorities and communities to act upon the warnings received. This involves training and resources to execute evacuation plans effectively.

Challenges in Implementation

Despite the theoretical framework, several challenges impede the effective implementation of EWS on Planet Nebula:

1. **Technological Limitations:** Many regions on Nebula lack the necessary infrastructure to support advanced monitoring technologies. Remote areas may struggle with connectivity, hindering real-time data transmission.

2. **Public Awareness and Education:** A significant barrier is the lack of awareness among the populace regarding the existence and importance of EWS. Without education on how to respond to alerts, the effectiveness of these systems diminishes.

3. **Coordination Among Agencies:** Effective EWS requires collaboration between various governmental and non-governmental organizations. Poor coordination can lead to misinformation and delayed responses.

4. **Cultural Factors:** Diverse cultural perceptions of risk can affect how communities respond to warnings. Some populations may be skeptical of alerts, leading to non-compliance during evacuations.

Examples of Effective Practices

On Planet Nebula, several regions have successfully implemented EWS and evacuation plans, serving as models for others:

- **The Coastal Region of Aquaria:** This area, prone to tsunamis, has established a robust EWS that includes a network of buoys equipped with sensors to detect changes in oceanic conditions. Upon detecting a potential tsunami, alerts are disseminated via text messages and public sirens, prompting immediate evacuations to higher ground.

- **The Mountainous Region of Terranova:** In response to frequent landslides, Terranova has developed a community-based EWS that trains local volunteers to monitor environmental changes. The system emphasizes local knowledge and rapid communication, enabling swift evacuations during heavy rainfall.

- **The Urban Center of Metropolis:** Metropolis has integrated technology into its EWS, employing an app that provides real-time alerts and evacuation routes based on users' locations.   This innovative approach has increased public engagement and compliance during emergencies.

Conclusion

In conclusion, the establishment of effective early warning systems and evacuation plans is paramount for enhancing disaster resilience on Planet Nebula.   While challenges remain, the integration of technology, community engagement, and inter-agency coordination can significantly improve the effectiveness of these systems. As Nebula continues to grapple with natural disasters, the lessons learned from successful practices can inform future governance reforms aimed at safeguarding its inhabitants.

Rehabilitation and reconstruction efforts

Rehabilitation and reconstruction efforts following a crisis are critical components of effective governance, particularly on Planet Nebula, where environmental challenges and natural disasters are frequent. This section explores the theoretical frameworks, practical challenges, and case studies related to these efforts, emphasizing the necessity for a holistic approach that integrates community involvement, sustainable practices, and efficient resource management.

Theoretical Frameworks

Theories of disaster recovery and resilience provide the foundation for understanding rehabilitation and reconstruction efforts. One prominent model is the **Disaster Recovery Framework**, which outlines phases of recovery, including:

+ **Immediate Response:** This phase focuses on addressing urgent needs, such as food, shelter, and medical care.

+ **Short-term Recovery:** In this phase, temporary solutions are implemented to restore basic services and infrastructure.

+ **Long-term Recovery:** This phase involves rebuilding communities and enhancing resilience to future disasters.

The **Resilience Theory** posits that communities with strong social networks and adaptive capacities are better equipped to recover from crises. This theory underscores the importance of local knowledge and participation in the rehabilitation process.

Challenges in Rehabilitation and Reconstruction

Despite theoretical frameworks, several challenges hinder effective rehabilitation and reconstruction efforts on Planet Nebula:

+ **Resource Allocation:** Limited financial and material resources can impede recovery efforts. Governments often struggle to prioritize funding between immediate needs and long-term investments.

+ **Coordination Among Stakeholders:** Effective rehabilitation requires collaboration between government agencies, non-governmental organizations (NGOs), and local communities. Poor coordination can lead to duplication of efforts or gaps in service provision.

+ **Cultural Sensitivity:** Reconstruction efforts must respect local customs and practices. Failure to do so can result in community resistance and hinder the success of recovery programs.

+ **Environmental Considerations:** Reconstruction efforts that do not account for environmental sustainability can exacerbate vulnerabilities to future disasters. For instance, rebuilding in flood-prone areas without adequate drainage systems can lead to repeated losses.

Case Studies of Rehabilitation Efforts

Several notable case studies from Planet Nebula illustrate the complexities of rehabilitation and reconstruction:

Case Study 1: The Great Nebulian Flood of 2045   In 2045, a catastrophic flood devastated several regions of Planet Nebula, displacing thousands and causing extensive damage to infrastructure. The rehabilitation efforts were guided by the principles of the Disaster Recovery Framework.

+ **Immediate Response:** Emergency shelters were established within 48 hours, providing essential services to affected populations.

+ **Short-term Recovery:** Temporary housing units were constructed, and local businesses were supported through micro-grants to stimulate economic activity.

+ **Long-term Recovery:** A comprehensive flood management system was developed, incorporating green infrastructure such as wetlands and permeable pavements to mitigate future flooding risks.

The success of these efforts was attributed to strong community engagement and the integration of local knowledge into the planning process.

Case Study 2: The Nebulian Wildfires of 2028 In 2028, wildfires swept through the Nebulian forests, prompting extensive rehabilitation efforts focused on ecological restoration and community resilience.

+ **Immediate Response:** Evacuation protocols were activated, and emergency services coordinated firefighting efforts.

+ **Short-term Recovery:** Affected residents received financial assistance and mental health support to cope with the trauma of displacement.

+ **Long-term Recovery:** The restoration of ecosystems involved reforestation initiatives and the establishment of firebreaks to protect communities from future wildfires. Educational programs were implemented to teach residents about fire prevention strategies.

This case highlighted the importance of integrating environmental considerations into rehabilitation efforts, ensuring that communities are not only rebuilt but also made more resilient to future crises.

Conclusion

Rehabilitation and reconstruction efforts on Planet Nebula are multifaceted processes that require a balance between immediate needs and long-term sustainability. The integration of theoretical frameworks, community engagement, and environmental considerations is essential for successful recovery. As Planet Nebula continues to face challenges from natural disasters, learning from past experiences and adapting strategies will be crucial in building resilient societies capable of withstanding future crises.

Climate Change Adaptation Policies

Climate change poses a significant threat to the stability and sustainability of societies across the universe, including Planet Nebula. As temperatures rise, precipitation patterns shift, and extreme weather events become more frequent, it is imperative that Nebulian policymakers adopt effective climate change adaptation strategies. This section explores the theoretical frameworks, challenges, and practical examples of climate change adaptation policies on Planet Nebula.

Theoretical Frameworks

Adaptation to climate change can be understood through various theoretical lenses, including ecological resilience theory and the socio-ecological systems framework.

Ecological Resilience Theory Ecological resilience theory posits that ecosystems have the capacity to absorb disturbances while maintaining their essential functions and structures. This theory can be applied to governance systems, suggesting that flexible and adaptive governance structures are crucial for responding to climate change impacts.

Socio-Ecological Systems Framework The socio-ecological systems framework emphasizes the interconnectedness of social and ecological systems. It highlights the need for policies that consider both human and environmental needs, fostering sustainable development.

These frameworks guide policymakers in designing comprehensive adaptation strategies that are context-specific and responsive to the unique challenges faced by different regions of Planet Nebula.

Challenges in Climate Change Adaptation

While the necessity for climate change adaptation policies is clear, several challenges hinder effective implementation:

1. Lack of Data and Research Many regions on Planet Nebula suffer from a lack of reliable climate data, making it difficult to assess vulnerabilities and design appropriate adaptation measures. Without robust data, policymakers may struggle to identify priority areas for intervention.

2. Economic Constraints Adapting to climate change often requires significant financial investment. Many Nebulian regions, particularly those that are economically disadvantaged, may lack the resources to implement necessary adaptation measures. This economic disparity can exacerbate existing inequalities.

3. Political Will and Governance Structures   Effective climate adaptation requires strong political will and governance structures that facilitate collaboration across various sectors and levels of government. In some cases, bureaucratic inertia and conflicting interests can impede progress.

4. Public Awareness and Engagement   Public understanding of climate change and its implications is crucial for successful adaptation. However, misinformation and lack of awareness can lead to public apathy or resistance to necessary changes.

Examples of Climate Change Adaptation Policies

Despite these challenges, several innovative adaptation policies have emerged on Planet Nebula, showcasing the potential for effective responses to climate change.

1. Coastal Resilience Initiatives   In coastal regions of Nebula, where rising sea levels threaten communities, local governments have implemented resilience initiatives that include the construction of sea walls, restoration of mangroves, and the establishment of buffer zones. These measures aim to protect infrastructure and ecosystems while enhancing community resilience.

2. Water Management Strategies   Given the increasing variability in precipitation patterns, water management has become a priority for many Nebulian societies. Policies promoting rainwater harvesting, the construction of reservoirs, and efficient irrigation practices have been adopted to ensure sustainable water supply, particularly in agricultural areas.

3. Climate-Resilient Agriculture   To address the impacts of climate change on food security, Nebulian governments have promoted climate-resilient agricultural practices. This includes the development of drought-resistant crop varieties, agroforestry systems, and sustainable land management practices that enhance soil health and reduce vulnerability to extreme weather events.

4. Urban Adaptation Plans   In urban centers, adaptation plans have been developed to enhance infrastructure resilience. This includes retrofitting buildings to withstand extreme weather, improving drainage systems to prevent flooding, and creating green spaces to mitigate urban heat effects.

Conclusion

Climate change adaptation policies on Planet Nebula are crucial for ensuring the sustainability and resilience of societies in the face of ongoing environmental challenges. By leveraging theoretical frameworks, addressing challenges, and implementing innovative strategies, Nebulian policymakers can foster a more adaptive and resilient future. Continued investment in research, public engagement, and cross-sector collaboration will be essential to overcoming barriers and enhancing the effectiveness of adaptation efforts.

$$\text{Adaptation Success} = f(\text{Data Quality, Economic Resources, Political Will, Public Engager}$$
$$\tag{49}$$

As represented in Equation (1), the success of adaptation policies is a function of multiple interrelated factors, emphasizing the need for a holistic approach to climate change adaptation on Planet Nebula.

Pandemic Response Strategies

Healthcare infrastructure and capacity building

The healthcare infrastructure of Planet Nebula has undergone significant transformations in response to various crises, particularly during the pandemic. The ability to effectively manage and respond to health emergencies hinges on robust healthcare systems that are well-equipped to handle surges in patient demand. This section explores the critical components of healthcare infrastructure and the importance of capacity building in ensuring a resilient health system.

Theoretical Framework

Healthcare infrastructure refers to the physical and organizational structures needed for the delivery of healthcare services. This includes hospitals, clinics, laboratories, and the workforce required to operate these facilities. Capacity building, on the other hand, involves enhancing the skills, competencies, and resources of healthcare providers and institutions to improve health outcomes.

The theoretical underpinnings of healthcare infrastructure can be framed through the lens of the Health Systems Framework (HSF), which emphasizes six building blocks: service delivery, health workforce, health information systems, medical products and technologies, financing, and governance. Each of these components plays a vital role in shaping the capacity of the healthcare system to respond to crises.

$$\text{Health System Capacity} = f(\text{Service Delivery, Workforce, Information Systems, Finan})$$
$$(50)$$

Challenges in Healthcare Infrastructure

Despite advancements, Nebula's healthcare infrastructure has faced numerous challenges:

* **Insufficient Facilities:** Many regions, particularly rural areas, lack adequate healthcare facilities. This disparity has resulted in unequal access to healthcare services, leading to poorer health outcomes for marginalized populations.

* **Workforce Shortages:** A significant shortage of healthcare professionals, particularly in specialized fields, has hampered the ability to provide timely and effective care. This issue is exacerbated by the brain drain, where skilled professionals migrate to other planets for better opportunities.

* **Inadequate Funding:** Funding for healthcare remains inconsistent, often reliant on fluctuating governmental budgets. This unpredictability hinders long-term planning and investment in essential infrastructure.

* **Technological Gaps:** The rapid pace of technological advancement has left some healthcare facilities struggling to keep up. Many hospitals lack access to the latest medical equipment and information technology systems, which are crucial for efficient patient care.

Capacity Building Initiatives

To address these challenges, Nebula has implemented several capacity-building initiatives aimed at strengthening its healthcare infrastructure:

* **Training Programs:** Government and non-governmental organizations have launched training programs for healthcare workers, focusing on both technical skills and leadership development. For example, the *Nebulian Health Workforce Initiative* has trained over 10,000 healthcare professionals in emergency response protocols.

- **Infrastructure Investments:** Significant investments have been made to expand healthcare facilities, particularly in underserved regions. The construction of the *Nebula Health Network*, a series of interconnected hospitals, has improved access to care for millions.

- **Public-Private Partnerships:** Collaborations between the government and private sector have facilitated the development of innovative solutions. For instance, partnerships with technology firms have led to the implementation of telemedicine services, allowing patients in remote areas to access healthcare professionals without the need for travel.

- **Community Engagement:** Engaging local communities in health initiatives has proven effective. Programs that train community health workers to provide basic healthcare services have been instrumental in bridging the gap between formal healthcare systems and the populations they serve.

Case Study: The Pandemic Response

The COVID-19 pandemic served as a critical test for Nebula's healthcare infrastructure. The government implemented a series of measures to bolster capacity:

- **Rapid Expansion of Testing Facilities:** In response to the surge in cases, the government established over 200 testing centers within weeks. This rapid expansion was facilitated by leveraging existing healthcare infrastructure and mobilizing resources from various sectors.

- **Surge Capacity Planning:** Hospitals developed surge capacity plans, which included the establishment of temporary treatment facilities and the reallocation of resources to high-demand areas. The *Nebulian Emergency Response Framework* was instrumental in coordinating these efforts.

- **Vaccine Distribution and Administration:** A comprehensive strategy for vaccine distribution was implemented, utilizing both public and private healthcare networks. The result was the successful inoculation of 80% of the eligible population within six months.

Conclusion

The healthcare infrastructure and capacity building on Planet Nebula are crucial for ensuring effective responses to health emergencies. While significant strides have been made, ongoing challenges necessitate continued investment and innovation. By addressing workforce shortages, enhancing facility capabilities, and fostering community engagement, Nebula can strengthen its healthcare system for future crises.

The lessons learned from the pandemic highlight the importance of preparedness and adaptability in healthcare infrastructure. As Nebula looks to the future, a commitment to sustainable capacity building will be essential for safeguarding public health and enhancing the resilience of its healthcare system.

Test, track, and trace strategies

The emergence of pandemics, such as the recent global health crisis, has underscored the importance of robust test, track, and trace strategies in managing public health. These strategies are crucial for identifying and mitigating the spread of infectious diseases, thereby safeguarding the health of the population.

Theoretical Framework

The theoretical underpinnings of test, track, and trace strategies can be traced back to epidemiological models that emphasize the importance of early detection and intervention. One of the foundational models is the SIR model, which categorizes the population into three compartments: Susceptible (S), Infected (I), and Recovered (R). The dynamics of disease spread can be represented by the following set of ordinary differential equations:

$$\frac{dS}{dt} = -\beta \frac{SI}{N} \tag{51}$$

$$\frac{dI}{dt} = \beta \frac{SI}{N} - \gamma I \tag{52}$$

$$\frac{dR}{dt} = \gamma I \tag{53}$$

Where: - β is the transmission rate, - γ is the recovery rate, and - N is the total population.

Incorporating test, track, and trace strategies into this model can significantly alter the dynamics of disease spread. By increasing the rate of testing, we can effectively reduce the number of susceptible individuals who become infected, thereby flattening the curve of infection.

Implementation Challenges

Despite the theoretical advantages, the implementation of test, track, and trace strategies faces several challenges:

- **Resource Allocation:** Adequate resources, including testing kits and trained personnel, are essential for effective implementation. During the initial phases of a pandemic, many regions faced shortages, leading to delayed responses.

- **Public Compliance:** The success of tracking and tracing relies heavily on public cooperation. Misinformation and distrust can lead to non-compliance with testing and reporting requirements, undermining the effectiveness of the strategy.

- **Data Privacy Concerns:** The collection and processing of personal data for tracking purposes raise significant privacy issues. Striking a balance between public health needs and individual privacy rights is a complex challenge.

Case Study: Nebula's Pandemic Response

Planet Nebula faced a significant health crisis due to the outbreak of the Nebulian Flu. The government implemented a comprehensive test, track, and trace strategy, which involved the following steps:

1. **Mass Testing Campaign:** The government launched a mass testing campaign, providing free testing kits to all citizens. This initiative was supported by a robust public awareness campaign to encourage participation.

2. **Digital Tracking Tools:** Nebula developed a mobile application that allowed citizens to voluntarily report their health status and receive alerts about potential exposure. The app utilized anonymized data to protect user privacy while enabling effective tracking.

3. **Contact Tracing Teams:** Trained teams of contact tracers were deployed to follow up with individuals who tested positive, identifying potential contacts and advising them on self-isolation and testing.

Outcomes and Lessons Learned

The implementation of these strategies yielded several important outcomes:

+ **Reduced Transmission Rates:** The combination of widespread testing and effective contact tracing resulted in a significant reduction in transmission rates, demonstrating the efficacy of early intervention.

+ **Public Engagement:** The government's transparent communication and emphasis on community health fostered public trust, leading to high participation rates in testing and tracking initiatives.

+ **Data Utilization:** The use of anonymized data for tracking purposes balanced public health needs with privacy concerns, setting a precedent for future health initiatives.

In conclusion, the test, track, and trace strategies employed on Planet Nebula serve as a model for other societies facing similar public health challenges. By prioritizing resource allocation, public engagement, and data privacy, governments can enhance their capacity to respond to pandemics effectively. Future governance reforms should incorporate these lessons to build resilient health systems capable of managing crises.

Coordination with international organizations

In the context of crisis management, particularly during pandemics, the coordination with international organizations plays a critical role in shaping effective response strategies. International organizations such as the World Health Organization (WHO), the United Nations (UN), and regional entities like the European Centre for Disease Prevention and Control (ECDC) provide essential frameworks, resources, and expertise that enhance national capacities to respond to crises.

Theoretical Framework

The theoretical underpinnings of coordination with international organizations can be analyzed through the lens of global governance theories, which emphasize the importance of multilateral cooperation in addressing transnational challenges. According to Keohane and Nye (1977), the concept of complex interdependence highlights how states are increasingly reliant on one another for resources, information, and policy solutions. This interdependence necessitates a collaborative approach to crisis management, where international organizations serve as platforms for negotiation, resource sharing, and capacity building.

Challenges in Coordination

Despite the theoretical advantages of coordination, several challenges hinder effective collaboration with international organizations:

- **Sovereignty Concerns:** Nations often prioritize their sovereignty, leading to reluctance in fully committing to international guidelines or assistance. This was evident during the initial stages of the COVID-19 pandemic, where some countries hesitated to share data or accept international aid due to fears of losing control over their health policies.

- **Resource Disparities:** Disparities in resources and capacities among countries can lead to unequal partnerships. Wealthier nations often dominate the agenda-setting process, which can marginalize the voices and needs of developing countries. This disparity was highlighted in the distribution of vaccines during the COVID-19 pandemic, where high-income countries secured a majority of the initial supplies, leaving lower-income nations struggling to access vaccines.

- **Bureaucratic Inefficiencies:** International organizations can suffer from bureaucratic delays and inefficiencies, which can impede timely responses. For example, the WHO faced criticism for its delayed response to the COVID-19 outbreak, which some attributed to its complex decision-making processes and the need for consensus among member states.

Successful Examples of Coordination

Despite these challenges, there are notable examples where coordination with international organizations has led to effective crisis management:

- **The Global Fund to Fight AIDS, Tuberculosis and Malaria:** This partnership between governments, civil society, and the private sector exemplifies successful coordination. By pooling resources and expertise, the Global Fund has significantly reduced mortality rates from these diseases in many countries, demonstrating the power of international collaboration.

- **The COVID-19 Vaccines Global Access (COVAX) Initiative:** COVAX is a global effort aimed at equitable access to COVID-19 vaccines. By bringing together governments, manufacturers, and international organizations, COVAX has sought to ensure that vaccines are distributed fairly, particularly to lower-income countries. As of mid-2023, COVAX has delivered millions of doses worldwide, showcasing the importance of coordinated efforts in a global health crisis.

+ **The International Health Regulations (IHR):** Established by the WHO, the IHR provides a legal framework for countries to report and respond to public health emergencies. The IHR has been instrumental in facilitating information sharing and coordinated responses to outbreaks, such as the Ebola virus outbreak in West Africa from 2014 to 2016, where rapid international response helped contain the spread.

Recommendations for Improved Coordination

To enhance coordination with international organizations in crisis management, several recommendations can be proposed:

+ **Strengthening Legal Frameworks:** Countries should be encouraged to adopt and implement international legal frameworks like the IHR more rigorously. This includes committing to transparent reporting of health data and adhering to international guidelines during crises.

+ **Enhancing Resource Sharing Mechanisms:** International organizations should work towards establishing more robust mechanisms for resource sharing, particularly for vulnerable nations. This could include emergency funds, medical supplies, and expertise to ensure that all countries are adequately prepared for crises.

+ **Fostering Trust and Collaboration:** Building trust among nations is essential for effective coordination. This can be achieved through regular dialogues, joint training exercises, and collaborative research initiatives that enhance mutual understanding and cooperation in crisis management.

In conclusion, while coordination with international organizations presents challenges, it remains a vital component of effective crisis management. By leveraging international frameworks, sharing resources, and fostering collaboration, nations can better prepare for and respond to crises, ultimately enhancing global health security.

Terrorism and National Security

Counterterrorism measures and intelligence gathering

In the complex landscape of governance on Planet Nebula, counterterrorism measures and intelligence gathering have become paramount in ensuring national security. The Nebulian government has adopted a multifaceted approach that integrates advanced technology, community engagement, and international collaboration to combat the threats posed by terrorism.

Theoretical Framework

Counterterrorism strategies can be analyzed through various theoretical lenses, including the Rational Choice Theory and the Social Movement Theory. Rational Choice Theory posits that individuals make decisions based on a cost-benefit analysis, suggesting that effective counterterrorism must alter the perceived benefits of engaging in terrorism. On the other hand, Social Movement Theory emphasizes the role of social structures and collective identity in motivating terrorist behavior. Understanding these theoretical frameworks allows policymakers to design more effective counterterrorism initiatives that address both the motivations behind terrorism and the operational capabilities of terrorist organizations.

Intelligence Gathering Techniques

Effective intelligence gathering is crucial for preempting terrorist activities. The Nebulian government employs a variety of techniques, including:

- **Human Intelligence (HUMINT):** This involves gathering information through interpersonal contact. Agents infiltrate groups suspected of terrorist activities to collect firsthand information.

- **Signals Intelligence (SIGINT):** The interception of communications, including phone calls and emails, allows intelligence agencies to monitor potential threats. This technique has raised ethical concerns regarding privacy rights, necessitating a delicate balance between security and civil liberties.

- **Geospatial Intelligence (GEOINT):** Utilizing satellite imagery and geographic information systems, the government can track movements and identify potential terrorist training camps or hideouts.

+ **Open Source Intelligence (OSINT):** Analysts sift through publicly available information, including social media, to detect patterns or signals of radicalization and recruitment.

Challenges in Intelligence Gathering

Despite the advanced techniques employed, several challenges hinder effective intelligence gathering:

+ **Information Overload:** The sheer volume of data collected can overwhelm analysts, leading to potential oversights. Effective filtering and prioritization systems are essential to manage this information overload.

+ **False Positives:** The risk of misidentifying innocent individuals as threats can lead to unjust actions and erode public trust in government institutions. The Nebulian government has implemented rigorous review processes to mitigate this risk.

+ **Interagency Coordination:** The effectiveness of counterterrorism efforts often depends on the seamless sharing of intelligence among various government agencies. Historical instances of poor coordination have resulted in missed opportunities to thwart attacks.

Counterterrorism Measures

The Nebulian government has implemented several counterterrorism measures, including:

+ **Legislative Framework:** Laws that enhance the powers of law enforcement agencies to conduct surveillance and apprehend suspects have been enacted. However, these laws are often met with public scrutiny and demands for transparency.

+ **Community Engagement Programs:** Recognizing that communities play a crucial role in preventing radicalization, the government has initiated programs aimed at fostering dialogue and trust between law enforcement and local populations. These programs help identify early signs of radicalization and promote community resilience against extremist ideologies.

+ **International Cooperation:** Terrorism is a global issue that transcends borders. The Nebulian government collaborates with international organizations and foreign governments to share intelligence and coordinate counterterrorism operations. Joint exercises and information-sharing agreements have proven effective in dismantling transnational terrorist networks.

Case Studies and Examples

Several notable cases illustrate the effectiveness of Nebulian counterterrorism measures:

+ **Operation Starfall:** In a coordinated effort involving HUMINT and SIGINT, Nebulian intelligence successfully thwarted a planned attack on a major public event. The operation involved the infiltration of a suspected terrorist cell, leading to the arrest of key operatives and the seizure of explosives.

+ **The Community Watch Initiative:** Launched in response to rising radicalization in urban areas, this initiative empowered local citizens to report suspicious activities. The program resulted in several arrests and a significant decrease in extremist recruitment in targeted neighborhoods.

Conclusion

Counterterrorism measures and intelligence gathering on Planet Nebula reflect a complex interplay of theory, technology, and community engagement. While challenges persist, the government's commitment to adapting its strategies and fostering collaboration—both domestically and internationally—has positioned Nebula as a proactive player in the global fight against terrorism. As the landscape of threats evolves, so too must the approaches to safeguarding the Nebulian populace, ensuring that security measures do not infringe upon the very liberties they aim to protect.

Civil liberties and privacy concerns

In the context of governance on Planet Nebula, the balance between national security and civil liberties has emerged as a contentious issue. As governments ramp up counterterrorism measures, there is a growing concern regarding the implications for individual rights and privacy. The tension between security and liberty is not a new phenomenon; it has been a central theme in political philosophy and public policy across various societies.

Theoretical Framework

The philosophical underpinnings of civil liberties can be traced back to Enlightenment thinkers such as John Locke and Jean-Jacques Rousseau, who emphasized the inherent rights of individuals and the social contract. Locke posited that individuals possess natural rights to life, liberty, and property, which governments must protect. Rousseau, on the other hand, argued for the importance of the general will and collective sovereignty, suggesting that individual freedoms are best safeguarded within the framework of a democratic society.

In contrast, the utilitarian perspective, championed by philosophers like Jeremy Bentham and John Stuart Mill, often prioritizes the greater good over individual rights. This perspective can lead to policies that infringe upon civil liberties in the name of security. The challenge for Nebulian governance lies in reconciling these competing philosophical viewpoints to create a framework that respects individual rights while effectively addressing security concerns.

Problems of Surveillance and Data Collection

The rise of surveillance technologies has significantly altered the landscape of civil liberties on Planet Nebula. Governments have increasingly employed advanced surveillance systems, including facial recognition technology, data mining, and mass data collection, ostensibly to enhance national security. However, these practices raise significant ethical and legal concerns.

$$\text{Privacy Loss} = \text{Surveillance Intensity} \times \text{Data Sensitivity} \qquad (54)$$

This equation illustrates that as surveillance intensity increases, the potential for privacy loss escalates, particularly when sensitive data is involved. For instance, the implementation of widespread facial recognition in public spaces has led to an erosion of anonymity, with citizens feeling constantly monitored. A survey conducted by the Nebulian Council for Civil Liberties found that 78% of respondents expressed discomfort with being surveilled in public spaces, highlighting a significant public backlash against invasive surveillance practices.

Furthermore, the legal frameworks governing data collection on Planet Nebula often lag behind technological advancements. Many citizens are unaware of how their data is collected, stored, and utilized, leading to a profound sense of mistrust in governmental institutions. This disconnect can be attributed to a lack of transparency and accountability in data handling practices.

Case Studies of Privacy Violations

Several high-profile cases have underscored the potential for abuse of power in the name of security on Planet Nebula. One notable incident involved the Nebulian Intelligence Agency (NIA), which was found to have conducted unauthorized surveillance on political activists and journalists. The revelations sparked widespread outrage and led to calls for reform in surveillance practices.

In another instance, a data breach at the Ministry of Security exposed the personal information of millions of Nebulians, raising alarms about data protection measures. The incident not only violated the privacy of individuals but also highlighted the vulnerabilities inherent in governmental data systems. The fallout from these breaches has prompted a national conversation about the need for stricter regulations governing data privacy and protection.

Balancing Security and Civil Liberties

The challenge for Nebulian governance lies in finding a balance between ensuring national security and protecting civil liberties. Policymakers must navigate the complexities of implementing effective security measures without infringing upon individual rights. This requires a multi-faceted approach that includes:

- **Clear Legal Frameworks:** Establishing comprehensive laws that define the limits of surveillance and data collection, ensuring that they are subject to judicial oversight.

- **Transparency and Accountability:** Implementing mechanisms for public oversight of surveillance practices, including regular reporting on data collection activities and their justifications.

- **Public Engagement:** Encouraging citizen participation in discussions about privacy and security, fostering a culture of informed consent regarding data practices.

- **Technological Safeguards:** Utilizing privacy-enhancing technologies to minimize data collection and ensure that personal information is adequately protected.

Conclusion

As Planet Nebula grapples with the complexities of governance in an increasingly interconnected world, the preservation of civil liberties amidst security concerns remains paramount. The philosophical debates surrounding individual rights and the role of government must inform policy decisions that seek to protect citizens while ensuring their safety. By prioritizing transparency, accountability, and public engagement, Nebulian governance can strive to create a society that values both security and individual freedoms, ultimately fostering a more just and equitable environment for all Nebulians.

International cooperation in combating terrorism

In an increasingly interconnected world, the phenomenon of terrorism transcends national borders, necessitating robust international cooperation to effectively address and mitigate its impacts. The complexities of global terrorism require a multifaceted approach that combines intelligence sharing, joint operations, and comprehensive legal frameworks. This section delves into the mechanisms, challenges, and successful examples of international collaboration in combating terrorism.

Theoretical Framework

Theoretical underpinnings of international cooperation in combating terrorism can be drawn from various disciplines, including international relations, security studies, and political science. The *Collective Security Theory* posits that nations can enhance their security by forming alliances to deter aggression, with the premise that an attack on one is an attack on all. This theory is particularly relevant in the context of terrorism, where the threat is diffuse and can emanate from any part of the globe.

Additionally, the *Network Theory* provides insights into how terrorist organizations operate. Terrorist networks often span multiple countries, making it imperative for states to collaborate. By understanding the interconnectedness of these networks, states can develop strategies to disrupt their operations through coordinated actions.

Challenges to International Cooperation

Despite the theoretical frameworks supporting collaboration, several challenges hinder effective international cooperation in combating terrorism:

- **Sovereignty Concerns:** Nations often prioritize their sovereignty, leading to reluctance in sharing sensitive intelligence or conducting joint operations. This can result in fragmented efforts that fail to address the global nature of terrorism.

- **Divergent Legal Frameworks:** Different countries have varying definitions of terrorism and associated legal frameworks. This divergence complicates extradition processes, joint investigations, and the prosecution of terrorists across borders.

- **Resource Disparities:** Not all nations have the same capabilities or resources to combat terrorism. Wealthier nations may have advanced technology and intelligence capabilities, while less affluent countries may struggle with basic law enforcement, leading to imbalances in cooperation.

- **Political Will:** Domestic political considerations can influence a country's willingness to engage in international cooperation. Governments may face pressure from constituents to adopt unilateral approaches, undermining collaborative efforts.

Mechanisms of Cooperation

To overcome these challenges, several mechanisms have been established to facilitate international cooperation:

- **Multilateral Agreements:** Treaties such as the *United Nations Global Counter-Terrorism Strategy* provide a framework for member states to collaborate on counter-terrorism efforts. These agreements often include provisions for intelligence sharing, capacity building, and coordinated responses.

- **Regional Organizations:** Entities like the *European Union (EU)* and the *African Union (AU)* have developed regional counter-terrorism strategies that promote cooperation among member states. For instance, the EU's *Counter-Terrorism Strategy* emphasizes information sharing and joint operations among member states.

- **Joint Task Forces:** Collaborative initiatives, such as the *Global Coalition Against Daesh*, exemplify effective international cooperation. This coalition, comprising over 80 countries, has conducted joint military operations, shared intelligence, and provided training to local forces in Iraq and Syria.

+ **Intelligence Sharing Platforms:** Platforms like the *FBI's Terrorist Screening Center* and the *Interpol's I-24/7 Network* facilitate real-time intelligence sharing among countries, enhancing the ability to track and apprehend terrorists.

Successful Examples of Cooperation

Several instances highlight the effectiveness of international cooperation in combating terrorism:

+ **The Capture of Abu Musab al-Zarqawi:** The coordination between the United States and Iraqi intelligence services led to the successful targeting and killing of al-Zarqawi, the leader of al-Qaeda in Iraq, in 2006. This operation was a result of extensive intelligence sharing and joint planning.

+ **The European Arrest Warrant:** This legal framework allows for the arrest and transfer of individuals suspected of terrorism across EU member states without the need for extradition processes. It has facilitated the swift apprehension of terrorists and has been instrumental in disrupting plots.

+ **The Joint Comprehensive Plan of Action (JCPOA):** Although primarily a nuclear agreement, the JCPOA includes provisions for addressing terrorism. The collaborative efforts among the P5+1 countries (China, France, Russia, the United Kingdom, the United States, and Germany) demonstrate how multilateral negotiations can extend beyond singular issues to encompass broader security concerns.

Conclusion

International cooperation in combating terrorism is not only necessary but also increasingly urgent in our globalized world. While challenges such as sovereignty concerns and resource disparities persist, the mechanisms established for collaboration provide a foundation for effective action. Successful examples of cooperation illustrate that when nations work together, they can achieve significant strides in countering terrorism. As the threat landscape continues to evolve, fostering robust international partnerships will be critical in ensuring the safety and security of societies across the globe.

$$T = \frac{C + D + R}{S} \tag{55}$$

where T represents the effectiveness of international cooperation in combating terrorism, C is the level of collaboration, D is the degree of shared intelligence, R is the resources allocated, and S denotes the sovereignty concerns of participating nations. This equation underscores the need for a balanced approach to enhance the effectiveness of counter-terrorism efforts globally.

The Future of Governance on Planet Nebula

The Future of Governance on Planet Nebula

The Future of Governance on Planet Nebula

As we look ahead to the future of governance on Planet Nebula, it is essential to consider the dynamic interplay of technological advancements, societal shifts, and environmental imperatives that will shape the Nebulian political landscape. The governance model that emerges will not only reflect the unique characteristics of Nebulian society but also serve as a case study for other civilizations grappling with similar challenges.

Technological Integration in Governance

One of the foremost trends influencing the future of governance on Planet Nebula is the integration of advanced technologies, particularly artificial intelligence (AI) and big data analytics, into decision-making processes. The adoption of AI-driven governance systems has the potential to enhance efficiency, improve public service delivery, and facilitate data-driven policy formulation.

Consider the equation that represents the relationship between data input and decision-making efficiency:

$$E = \frac{D}{T} \tag{56}$$

where E is the efficiency of decision-making, D is the amount of data processed, and T is the time taken to reach a decision. As the volume of data increases, the potential for improved efficiency grows exponentially, provided that the algorithms used are transparent and accountable.

However, the reliance on AI also raises significant ethical concerns. Issues surrounding bias in algorithms, data privacy, and the potential for surveillance state dynamics must be addressed. The Nebulian government will need to establish robust legal frameworks and ethical guidelines to navigate these challenges. For instance, the implementation of the *Nebulian AI Ethics Charter* could serve as a foundational document outlining the principles of fairness, accountability, and transparency in AI governance.

Environmental Sustainability and Governance

Another critical factor shaping the future of governance on Planet Nebula is the pressing need for environmental sustainability. As climate change continues to pose existential threats, Nebulian leaders must prioritize eco-centric policies that promote sustainable development. This can be encapsulated in the following sustainability equation:

$$S = \frac{R + E + S}{C} \tag{57}$$

where S represents sustainability, R is resource management, E is environmental protection, S is social equity, and C is economic growth. The challenge lies in achieving a balance where all these components coexist harmoniously, ensuring that economic growth does not come at the expense of environmental degradation.

The Nebulian government has already initiated policies such as the *Green Initiative Program*, which aims to transition to renewable energy sources and implement sustainable agricultural practices. These initiatives could be expanded through international cooperation with other planets facing similar environmental challenges, creating a planetary alliance for sustainability.

Demographic Shifts and Social Dynamics

The demographic landscape of Planet Nebula is also evolving, with increasing diversity and shifting social dynamics. The rise of younger, more technologically-savvy populations demands a rethinking of traditional governance structures. Engaging these demographics through participatory governance models will be crucial.

One potential model is the *Digital Democracy Framework*, which leverages technology to facilitate citizen engagement in the policymaking process. This framework can be expressed as:

$$P = C + T + E \tag{58}$$

where P is participatory governance, C is citizen engagement, T is technological facilitation, and E is educational outreach. By fostering an environment where citizens feel empowered to contribute to governance, Nebula can cultivate a more inclusive and responsive political system.

Challenges Ahead

Despite these promising developments, the future of governance on Planet Nebula is fraught with challenges. The potential for technocracy to overshadow democratic processes, the risk of environmental catastrophes, and the need for social cohesion in an increasingly diverse society are all pressing issues.

To mitigate these challenges, Nebulian leaders must adopt a proactive approach that emphasizes resilience and adaptability. This could involve regular assessments of governance effectiveness, incorporating feedback from citizens, and remaining flexible to adjust policies in response to changing circumstances.

In conclusion, the future of governance on Planet Nebula holds immense potential for innovation and progress. By embracing technological advancements, prioritizing environmental sustainability, and fostering inclusive participation, Nebulian society can navigate the complexities of the 21st century and beyond. The lessons learned from Nebula's governance evolution may well serve as a beacon for other societies striving to create a more equitable and sustainable future.

Emerging trends and challenges

Technological advancements and their impact on governance

The integration of technological advancements into governance frameworks has transformed the landscape of public administration on Planet Nebula. As societies evolve, so too do the tools available for governance, which can lead to enhanced efficiency, transparency, and citizen engagement. However, these advancements also present significant challenges that require careful consideration and management.

Theoretical Framework

The impact of technology on governance can be understood through the lens of several theoretical frameworks, including the *Technological Determinism* theory, which posits that technology shapes societal structures and cultural values. This perspective suggests that technological innovations, such as artificial intelligence (AI) and big data analytics, fundamentally alter how governments operate and interact with citizens. Conversely, the *Social Construction of Technology* (SCOT) theory argues that social forces and human actions shape technological development, emphasizing that the implementation of technology in governance is not merely a technical decision but also a social one.

Efficiency and Automation

One of the most significant impacts of technological advancements on governance is the potential for increased efficiency through automation. For instance, the use of AI-driven algorithms in decision-making processes can streamline administrative tasks, reduce human error, and enhance service delivery. Consider the implementation of AI in public service departments, which can analyze vast amounts of data to optimize resource allocation. The equation governing this optimization can be represented as:

$$\text{Optimal Resource Allocation} = \frac{\sum_{i=1}^{n} \text{Data}_i \cdot \text{Weight}_i}{\sum_{i=1}^{n} \text{Weight}_i} \tag{59}$$

where Data_i represents the relevant data points and Weight_i denotes the importance assigned to each data point.

Transparency and Accountability

Technological advancements also foster greater transparency and accountability in governance. The introduction of blockchain technology, for instance, has the potential to revolutionize how government transactions are recorded and verified. By providing a decentralized and immutable ledger, blockchain can enhance public trust by ensuring that government actions are transparent and traceable. As noted by scholars, "the application of blockchain in public administration can mitigate corruption and increase citizen confidence in governmental institutions" [?].

Challenges of Implementation

Despite the benefits, the implementation of technology in governance is fraught with challenges. One significant issue is the digital divide, which refers to the gap between those who have access to digital technologies and those who do not. This divide can exacerbate existing inequalities, as marginalized communities may lack the resources to engage with digital governance platforms effectively. Furthermore, reliance on technology can lead to the erosion of human oversight in decision-making, raising ethical concerns about accountability and bias in AI algorithms.

Public Engagement and Participation

Technological advancements also reshape citizen engagement in governance. Social media platforms and online forums provide citizens with unprecedented opportunities to participate in the political process. For example, the use of digital platforms for public consultations allows governments to gather feedback from a broader demographic, fostering a more inclusive approach to policy-making. However, the rise of misinformation and echo chambers on these platforms poses significant risks to informed public discourse.

Case Studies: Successful Implementations

Several examples from Planet Nebula illustrate the successful integration of technology in governance. The Nebulian city of Auroria implemented a smart city initiative that utilizes the Internet of Things (IoT) to manage urban infrastructure. Sensors installed throughout the city collect data on traffic patterns, waste management, and energy consumption, enabling real-time adjustments to improve efficiency and sustainability. This initiative has resulted in a 30% reduction in energy consumption and a significant decrease in traffic congestion [?].

In another instance, the Nebulian government adopted a digital identity system that streamlines access to public services. Citizens can now authenticate their identity online, reducing wait times and improving service delivery. This system has increased citizen satisfaction with government services by 40% [?].

Conclusion

In conclusion, technological advancements have the potential to significantly impact governance on Planet Nebula, offering opportunities for increased efficiency, transparency, and citizen engagement. However, these benefits must be balanced against the challenges of implementation, including the digital divide and ethical concerns surrounding AI and data privacy. As Nebula continues to navigate these complexities, the lessons learned from both successful and unsuccessful implementations will be crucial in shaping the future of governance in an increasingly digital world.

Climate Change and Environmental Sustainability

The issue of climate change has emerged as one of the most pressing challenges facing societies across the universe, including the inhabitants of Planet Nebula. As a planet characterized by its diverse ecosystems and unique geographical features, Nebula is not immune to the adverse effects of climate change. This section explores the implications of climate change on environmental sustainability, the theoretical frameworks that guide governance responses, the problems faced by Nebulian society, and examples of initiatives aimed at mitigating these challenges.

Theoretical Frameworks

To understand the governance of climate change on Planet Nebula, we can draw upon several theoretical frameworks that have been developed in the field of environmental governance.   Notably, the **Sustainable Development Theory** emphasizes the need for a balance between economic growth, social equity, and environmental protection. This theory posits that sustainable development can only be achieved when all three pillars are considered in policy-making.

Furthermore, the **Ecological Modernization Theory** suggests that economic development   and   environmental   protection   can   be   reconciled   through technological innovation and the adoption of green technologies. This perspective is particularly relevant for Nebula, where technological advancements are crucial for addressing the challenges posed by climate change.

Problems Associated with Climate Change

The impact of climate change on Planet Nebula is multifaceted, affecting various sectors and communities. Some of the key problems include:

+ **Rising Temperatures:** Average temperatures on Nebula have increased by $\Delta T = 2.5°C$ over the past three decades, leading to altered weather patterns and increased frequency of extreme weather events.

+ **Biodiversity Loss:** The unique ecosystems of Nebula are under threat, with species extinction rates rising as habitats are destroyed or altered due to climate change. The loss of biodiversity disrupts ecological balance and can have cascading effects on food security and health.

+ **Water Scarcity:** Changes in precipitation patterns have resulted in severe droughts in some regions and flooding in others. The availability of fresh water, a critical resource for both agriculture and human consumption, is increasingly jeopardized.

+ **Economic Disruption:** Key industries, such as agriculture and tourism, face significant risks due to climate variability. For example, crop yields have decreased by $\Delta Y = 15\%$ in regions most affected by droughts and floods, leading to economic instability and food insecurity.

Examples of Initiatives for Environmental Sustainability

In response to these pressing challenges, the government of Planet Nebula has implemented a variety of initiatives aimed at promoting environmental sustainability. Some notable examples include:

1. **Renewable Energy Transition:** The Nebulian government has committed to generating **50%** of its energy from renewable sources by the year 2030. Investments in solar, wind, and geothermal energy have increased, resulting in a **30%** reduction in greenhouse gas emissions since 2020.

2. **Reforestation Programs:** Recognizing the importance of forests in carbon sequestration, Nebula has launched extensive reforestation programs aimed at restoring **1 million hectares** of deforested land by 2040. These initiatives not only contribute to carbon neutrality but also enhance biodiversity and protect watersheds.

3. **Sustainable Agriculture Practices:** To combat food insecurity while minimizing environmental impact, Nebula has promoted sustainable agricultural practices, such as organic farming and permaculture. These methods have led to an increase in soil health and a reduction in the use of chemical fertilizers by **40%** over the past five years.

4. **Public Awareness Campaigns:** The government has initiated public awareness campaigns focusing on the importance of individual actions in combating climate change. These campaigns have successfully increased community engagement, with **over 60%** of citizens participating in local sustainability initiatives.

Conclusion

In conclusion, climate change represents a significant threat to the environmental sustainability of Planet Nebula. The challenges posed by rising temperatures, biodiversity loss, water scarcity, and economic disruption necessitate a comprehensive and coordinated governance response. By leveraging theoretical frameworks such as Sustainable Development Theory and Ecological Modernization Theory, Nebula can navigate the complexities of climate governance. Through targeted initiatives aimed at renewable energy, reforestation, sustainable agriculture, and public engagement, the planet can work towards a more sustainable future, ensuring the well-being of both current and future generations.

Shifting demographics and social dynamics

The demographics of Planet Nebula are undergoing significant changes, driven by a confluence of factors including migration, aging populations, and evolving cultural identities. These shifts present both opportunities and challenges for governance, as policymakers must adapt to a rapidly changing social landscape.

Demographic Changes

One of the most pressing demographic changes on Planet Nebula is the increasing diversity of its population. As individuals from various cultural backgrounds migrate to urban centers in search of better economic opportunities, the social fabric of Nebulian society becomes increasingly complex. This phenomenon can be analyzed through the lens of *multiculturalism theory*, which posits that diverse cultural identities can coexist harmoniously, contributing to a richer social experience.

However, the reality often diverges from this ideal. For instance, the influx of migrants has led to tensions in some communities, where long-standing residents express concerns over job competition and cultural dilution. This situation has sparked debates about the balance between preserving cultural heritage and embracing multiculturalism, leading to calls for policies that promote integration without erasing individual identities.

Aging Population

Another critical demographic trend is the aging population of Nebula. As advancements in healthcare and living conditions extend life expectancy, the proportion of elderly citizens is increasing. According to the Nebulian Statistical Agency (NSA), the percentage of citizens aged 65 and older is projected to rise from 15% in 2023 to 25% by 2040. This demographic shift poses significant challenges for the healthcare system, pension schemes, and workforce dynamics.

The *dependency ratio*, defined as the ratio of dependents (aged 0-14 and 65+) to the working-age population (aged 15-64), is a crucial metric for understanding the implications of an aging population. The equation for the dependency ratio (DR) can be expressed as:

$$DR = \frac{D}{W} \times 100$$

where D represents the number of dependents and W represents the working-age population. As the dependency ratio increases, the economic burden on the working-age population intensifies, necessitating reforms in pension systems and healthcare delivery models.

Social Dynamics and Inequality

The shifting demographics also exacerbate existing social inequalities. As various demographic groups vie for resources, opportunities, and representation, disparities in wealth, education, and access to services become more pronounced. For example, the Progressive Coalition, a key political faction, has advocated for policies aimed at addressing income inequality through progressive taxation and social safety nets.

Despite these efforts, challenges remain. The rise of populist movements, often fueled by economic disenfranchisement, has led to increased polarization within society. The Conservative Movement has capitalized on these sentiments, promoting a narrative that positions certain demographic groups as threats to the social order. This rhetoric can undermine social cohesion and hinder collaborative governance.

Civic Engagement and Representation

As demographics shift, so too does the landscape of civic engagement. Younger, more diverse populations are increasingly participating in political processes, demanding representation and accountability from their leaders. Grassroots movements have emerged, focusing on issues such as climate change, social justice, and economic reform. These movements are often facilitated by digital platforms that enable rapid mobilization and communication.

However, the effectiveness of civic engagement is contingent upon the willingness of established political institutions to adapt. The Nebulian government has faced criticism for its slow response to emerging social dynamics, with many citizens feeling that their voices are not adequately represented in decision-making processes. This disconnect can lead to apathy and disillusionment, further complicating the governance landscape.

Conclusion

In conclusion, the shifting demographics and social dynamics of Planet Nebula present both challenges and opportunities for governance. Policymakers must navigate the complexities of multiculturalism, an aging population, and rising social inequalities to foster a cohesive and inclusive society. By embracing innovative governance approaches that prioritize representation and civic engagement, Nebula can harness the strengths of its diverse population to build a more resilient future.

The lessons learned from Nebula's evolving demographics can serve as valuable insights for other societies grappling with similar issues, emphasizing the need for adaptive governance that reflects the realities of a changing world.

Lessons from Nebula's Policy Shifts

Successes and failures of different governance approaches

The governance landscape of Planet Nebula has been characterized by a series of transformative approaches, each with its own set of successes and failures. This section delves into the key governance models adopted on Nebula, evaluating their effectiveness through theoretical frameworks and real-world implications.

Decentralized Governance: The Tribal Era

The early governance system on Planet Nebula was rooted in decentralized tribal leadership, which allowed for localized decision-making. This model, while fostering community engagement, faced significant challenges. The theory of *collective action* suggests that decentralized systems can enhance participation but may also lead to fragmentation and conflict among tribes [?].

$$C = \frac{N(N-1)}{2} \tag{60}$$

Where C is the number of conflicts, and N is the number of tribes. As the equation illustrates, the potential for conflict increases exponentially with the number of decentralized units. This was evident during territorial disputes, which often escalated into violent confrontations, undermining social cohesion.

Centralized Monarchy: A Double-Edged Sword

The transition to a centralized monarchy marked a significant shift in governance, aiming to unify the diverse tribes under a single authority. While this approach brought about stability and a coherent legal framework, it also stifled local autonomy and led to widespread discontent. The *social contract theory* posits that citizens surrender certain freedoms in exchange for security and order [?]. However, when the monarchy failed to deliver on its promises, the legitimacy of its rule was called into question.

Democracy: The Double-Edged Sword of Participation

The democratic revolution on Nebula introduced a more participatory governance model, with the establishment of democratic institutions. Initially, this shift was celebrated as a triumph of citizen empowerment. The *participatory governance theory* emphasizes the importance of citizen involvement in decision-making processes, leading to more representative outcomes [?].

However, the implementation of democracy also revealed significant challenges. Voter apathy and manipulation by powerful interest groups undermined the integrity of elections. The concept of *political efficacy*—the belief that one's participation can influence political outcomes—suffered as citizens became disillusioned with the system. This disillusionment was exacerbated by the rise of populism, which often leveraged societal divisions for electoral gain.

Technocratic Governance: A Data-Driven Dilemma

In the Technocratic Era, Nebula embraced scientific expertise and data-driven policies. This approach aimed to enhance efficiency and effectiveness in governance. The *rational choice theory* suggests that decisions made based on empirical data can lead to optimal outcomes [?]. However, the reliance on data also sparked public skepticism, particularly regarding the transparency and ethical implications of algorithm-driven decision-making.

For instance, the implementation of AI algorithms in policy formulation raised concerns about bias and accountability. The following equation represents the potential for algorithmic bias:

$$B = \frac{D_i}{D_t} \times 100 \tag{61}$$

Where B is the bias percentage, D_i is the number of biased decisions made, and D_t is the total decisions made. As bias in algorithms became apparent, public trust in technocratic governance eroded, leading to calls for greater oversight and ethical standards.

The Hybrid Model: A Path Forward?

In recent years, Nebula has attempted to integrate elements from various governance models, creating a hybrid system that seeks to balance centralized authority with local autonomy. This approach draws on the principles of *adaptive governance*, which emphasizes flexibility and responsiveness to changing societal needs [?].

The successes of this hybrid model include enhanced citizen engagement through grassroots movements and increased responsiveness to social issues. However, challenges remain, particularly in managing the tensions between different political factions and ensuring equitable representation.

Lessons Learned

The examination of governance approaches on Planet Nebula reveals critical lessons applicable to other societies:

1. **Decentralization vs. Centralization**: While decentralized systems can foster engagement, they risk fragmentation. Centralized governance can provide stability but may suppress local voices.

2. **Democracy's Fragility**: Democratic systems require ongoing citizen engagement and vigilance against manipulation. The health of democracy is contingent upon the public's belief in its efficacy.

3. **Data-Driven Governance**: Technocratic approaches must prioritize transparency and ethical considerations to maintain public trust. The integration of technology should not come at the expense of accountability.

4. **Hybrid Governance**: A flexible, hybrid model that incorporates diverse governance strategies may offer a path to resilience, allowing societies to adapt to emerging challenges.

In conclusion, the successes and failures of governance approaches on Planet Nebula underscore the complexities of managing diverse societies. As Nebula navigates its future, the lessons learned from its past will be crucial in shaping effective and inclusive governance.

Policy implications for other societies

The governance evolution on Planet Nebula offers a wealth of insights and lessons that can be applied to other societies grappling with similar challenges. The Nebulian experience highlights the importance of adaptability, inclusivity, and the integration of technology in governance. This section will explore several key policy implications derived from Nebula's policy shifts, emphasizing how they may inform governance practices in diverse contexts.

Emphasizing Inclusivity in Governance

One of the most critical lessons from Nebula's transition from a centralized monarchy to a more democratic system is the necessity of inclusivity in governance. The Nebulian democratic revolution, while initially successful, faced significant challenges due to the exclusion of marginalized groups. This exclusion often led to social unrest and a lack of trust in institutions.

$$\text{Inclusivity Index} = \frac{\text{Number of marginalized groups represented}}{\text{Total number of groups}} \times 100 \quad (62)$$

Other societies can learn from this by actively ensuring that all segments of the population are represented in decision-making processes. Implementing policies that foster representation, such as proportional representation in electoral systems or dedicated seats for marginalized communities, can enhance social cohesion and trust in governance.

Balancing Technocracy and Democracy

Nebula's Technocratic Era demonstrated the potential benefits of integrating scientific expertise into policy-making. However, it also revealed the pitfalls of over-reliance on technocratic governance, particularly the erosion of public trust.

$$\text{Trust Level} = \frac{\text{Number of citizens who trust government}}{\text{Total population}} \times 100 \quad (63)$$

This balance can be achieved by establishing frameworks that allow for public input in technocratic decision-making processes. For example, creating citizen advisory boards that work alongside technocrats can ensure that policies are not only data-driven but also resonate with the values and needs of the community.

Addressing Economic Inequality

The Nebulian experience with economic policy reforms, particularly the privatization of key industries, underscores the importance of addressing income inequality. As Nebula embraced market capitalism, income disparities widened, leading to social discontent.

$$\text{Gini Coefficient} = \frac{A}{A + B} \quad (64)$$

Where A is the area between the Lorenz curve and the line of equality, and B is the area under the Lorenz curve.

To mitigate such issues, other societies should consider implementing robust social safety nets and progressive taxation systems that redistribute wealth effectively. Policies such as universal basic income (UBI) or enhanced welfare programs can provide a buffer against the adverse effects of economic reforms.

Prioritizing Environmental Sustainability

Nebula's transition to a green economy offers valuable lessons for other societies facing climate change challenges. The emphasis on renewable energy sources and sustainable development policies is crucial in creating resilient societies.

$$\text{Sustainability Index} = \frac{\text{Renewable energy consumption}}{\text{Total energy consumption}} \times 100 \quad (65)$$

Other nations can adopt similar frameworks by investing in renewable energy technologies and encouraging sustainable practices across all sectors. Policymakers should prioritize environmental education and incentivize businesses to adopt sustainable practices through tax breaks and grants.

Strengthening Crisis Management Frameworks

Nebula's experience with crisis management, particularly during natural disasters and pandemics, highlights the necessity for robust emergency response frameworks. The establishment of early warning systems and comprehensive rehabilitation plans proved essential in mitigating the impacts of crises.

$$\text{Crisis Response Efficiency} = \frac{\text{Number of successful interventions}}{\text{Total crises}} \times 100 \quad (66)$$

Other societies should invest in training programs for emergency responders and develop multi-agency coordination strategies to enhance their crisis response capabilities. Furthermore, integrating technology, such as AI and big data analytics, can improve predictive capabilities and enhance preparedness.

Fostering Citizen Engagement

The Nebulian political landscape demonstrated the power of grassroots movements and citizen activism in shaping policy. Engaging citizens in the political process fosters a sense of ownership and accountability.

$$\text{Engagement Rate} = \frac{\text{Number of active participants}}{\text{Eligible voters}} \times 100 \qquad (67)$$

Other societies can enhance citizen engagement by creating platforms for public discourse, such as town hall meetings and online forums. Encouraging civic education and participation in local governance can empower citizens and strengthen democratic processes.

Learning from Policy Failures

Finally, Nebula's policy shifts illustrate the importance of learning from past failures. The challenges faced during the implementation of democratic institutions and economic reforms provide valuable insights into the complexities of governance.

$$\text{Failure Rate} = \frac{\text{Number of failed policies}}{\text{Total policies implemented}} \times 100 \qquad (68)$$

Other societies should adopt a culture of reflection and adaptability, where policies are regularly assessed for effectiveness, and adjustments are made based on empirical evidence and public feedback. Establishing independent review bodies can facilitate this process and ensure transparency.

Conclusion

In conclusion, the governance experiences of Planet Nebula offer a rich tapestry of lessons for other societies. By emphasizing inclusivity, balancing technocracy with democratic engagement, addressing economic inequality, prioritizing environmental sustainability, strengthening crisis management, fostering citizen engagement, and learning from past failures, other societies can navigate their own governance challenges more effectively. The key takeaway is that governance is not a one-size-fits-all model; rather, it requires continuous adaptation and a willingness to learn from both successes and failures in the pursuit of a more equitable and sustainable future.

Recommendations for future governance reforms

In analyzing the governance shifts on Planet Nebula, several key recommendations emerge to guide future reforms. These recommendations are grounded in the lessons learned from Nebula's historical experiences and the evolving dynamics of its political, social, and economic landscapes. The following sections outline these recommendations, supported by relevant theories and examples from both Nebula and analogous societies.

Embrace Adaptive Governance Models

Governance on Planet Nebula has often struggled with rigidity in its institutions, leading to inefficiencies and public disillusionment. To counteract this, it is essential to adopt adaptive governance models that prioritize flexibility and responsiveness to change. Adaptive governance, as articulated by Folke et al. (2005), emphasizes the importance of learning and adaptation in policy-making processes.

$$\text{Adaptive Governance} = f(\text{Flexibility, Learning, Stakeholder Engagement}) \quad (69)$$

For instance, the implementation of participatory budgeting in various Earth cities, such as Porto Alegre in Brazil, has demonstrated how involving citizens in financial decision-making can lead to more responsive governance. Nebula could benefit from similar initiatives that empower local communities to influence budgetary allocations, ensuring that resources are directed toward pressing local needs.

Strengthen Democratic Institutions and Citizen Engagement

The rise of democracy on Nebula has been met with challenges, including political apathy and skepticism towards elected officials.   To revitalize democratic engagement, it is crucial to strengthen democratic institutions and foster a culture of civic participation.

$$\text{Civic Engagement} = \frac{\text{Informed Citizens} \times \text{Accessible Institutions}}{\text{Political Apathy}} \quad (70)$$

Implementing civic education programs that inform citizens about their rights and responsibilities, as well as the workings of government, can enhance public engagement. For example, the success of the "Civics for All" initiative in Canada, which aims to educate young citizens about democratic processes, could serve as a model for Nebula.

Promote Social Equity Through Inclusive Policies

Nebula's economic policies have often exacerbated income inequality, leading to social unrest and dissatisfaction. To address this, future governance reforms must prioritize social equity by implementing inclusive policies that ensure fair distribution of resources and opportunities.

$$\text{Social Equity} = \frac{\text{Access to Resources}}{\text{Systemic Barriers}} \tag{71}$$

The introduction of progressive taxation and robust social safety nets, akin to the Nordic model, can mitigate income disparities. Nebula should consider establishing a universal basic income (UBI) pilot program to evaluate its effectiveness in reducing poverty and promoting economic stability.

Leverage Technology for Transparent Governance

The Technocratic Era on Nebula highlighted the potential of data-driven governance, yet it also raised concerns about transparency and accountability. To harness technology effectively, governance reforms should focus on enhancing transparency through open data initiatives and digital platforms that facilitate public access to information.

$$\text{Transparency} = \frac{\text{Open Data Initiatives}}{\text{Corruption}} \tag{72}$$

For example, the implementation of open government platforms in countries like Estonia has transformed public service delivery and increased trust in government. Nebula can adopt similar technologies to provide citizens with real-time access to governmental data, thereby fostering accountability and trust.

Address Climate Change through Sustainable Policies

As Nebula grapples with the impacts of climate change, future governance must prioritize sustainability in all policy areas. This involves integrating environmental considerations into economic and social policies, promoting renewable energy, and enhancing climate resilience.

$$\text{Sustainable Governance} = f(\text{Environmental Policies, Economic Incentives, Community In} \tag{73}$$

The establishment of a Green New Deal, inspired by initiatives in various Earth nations, could serve as a comprehensive framework for addressing climate change while creating jobs and promoting economic growth. This approach would not only address environmental concerns but also stimulate the economy through investment in green technologies.

Foster International Cooperation and Global Governance

Given the interconnectedness of global challenges, Nebula must recognize the importance of international cooperation in governance. Future reforms should aim to strengthen diplomatic relations and participate actively in global governance frameworks that address issues such as climate change, trade, and security.

$$\text{Global Cooperation} = \frac{\text{International Treaties} + \text{Bilateral Agreements}}{\text{Nationalism}} \quad (74)$$

Engagement in international organizations, such as the Intergalactic Council for Sustainable Development, can provide Nebula with valuable insights and resources to tackle its challenges collaboratively. By fostering a spirit of cooperation, Nebula can position itself as a proactive player on the interstellar stage.

Continuous Evaluation and Reform of Policies

Finally, the governance landscape on Planet Nebula should be characterized by a commitment to continuous evaluation and reform of policies. Establishing mechanisms for regular review and feedback can help identify areas for improvement and ensure that policies remain relevant to the needs of the population.

$$\text{Policy Evaluation} = \frac{\text{Feedback Mechanisms} \times \text{Stakeholder Input}}{\text{Resistance to Change}} \quad (75)$$

Implementing a framework for policy audits, similar to the performance evaluation systems used in various Earth governments, can facilitate this process. By institutionalizing feedback loops, Nebula can create a governance structure that is both dynamic and responsive to the evolving needs of its society.

In conclusion, the future of governance on Planet Nebula hinges on the ability to adapt to changing circumstances and the willingness to learn from past experiences. By embracing these recommendations, Nebula can cultivate a more inclusive, transparent, and sustainable governance system that meets the needs of its diverse population while addressing the challenges of the 21st century and beyond.

Index

Milton Keynes UK
Ingram Content Group UK Ltd.
UKHW030743121124
451094UK00013B/1006

9 781779 666178